FANSHEN

by the same author

SLAG

THE GREAT EXHIBITION

KNUCKLE

TEETH 'N' SMILES

PLENTY

LICKING HITLER
(a play for television)

with Howard Brenton
BRASSNECK
(Methuen)

Fanshen

A play by
DAVID HARE

based on the book by
WILLIAM HINTON

FABER & FABER
London · Boston

First published in 1976
by Faber and Faber Limited
3 Queen Square London WC1
Reprinted 1980
Printed in Great Britain by
Latimer Trend & Company Ltd Plymouth
All rights reserved

ISBN 0 571 11019 3

Author's Preface

In 1948 George Orwell wrote: 'When you are on a sinking ship, your thoughts will be about sinking ships.' No one has put the modern writer's difficulty better. European literature of the last seventy years annotates the decline of the West, both in theory and in practice. Nearly every outstanding piece of writing since 1900 belongs to a culture of dissent. Writers have been trapped in negatives, forced back into sniping and objection, or into the lurid colours of their private imaginations. At some stage they will have to offer positive models for change, or their function will decay as irrevocably as the society they seek to describe.

In the summer of 1974 Max Stafford-Clark and William Gaskill asked me to read William Hinton's great book *Fanshen* and to dramatize it for the Joint Stock Theatre Group. They had just directed *The Speakers* from Heathcote Williams' book and were keen to set to work on another book through a long exploratory period of workshop and rehearsal.

The book's strength lies in its detail and the comprehensiveness of its many approaches to the one small village of Long Bow. Hinton is a polymath. Like a nineteenth-century novelist he makes it his business to know a good deal about everything: about politics, economics, medicine, military strategy, the law, history, agriculture, literature. He has mastered each discipline separately in order to present the lives of his subjects as fully as possible. Our aim could never be to cover Hinton's ground. We knew too little. We could only choose and then present one of the many plays that the book contains. The initial workshop period centred round the question: which one?

Together we broke down the possibilities—a play about the work team, a play about the outbreak of revolution, or maybe a play about a single character. But the final text is mine alone, and so, it proved, was the choice about which play to write. It is a play for Europe, for the West. Besides trying to explain as deftly as possible the aim and operation of land reform in China, to show how it changed men's souls as well as their bodies, the play is much concerned with political leadership, with the relationship in *any* society between leadership and led. In the political climate of Europe where the distrust between the people and their bureaucracy is now so profound, this seemed a subject of extreme urgency. For *Fanshen* seeks to explain to an audience who have no real experience of change what exactly that change might involve and how it can in practice be effected.

There are some essential principles for those of you who want to mount the work. Obviously, read the book. Although the play can be read instructively and is complete in itself, any production will quickly find that the play assumes an enormous sub-text which you can only explore through Hinton's original. One or two of the characters in the play are invented, or so changed as to be unrecognizable. For instance the assertive Ch'i-Yun in the play is quite different from the shy interpreter in Hinton's book. But by and large you will find the people there and in much more detail than I can offer.

And you will find the things—descriptions of *k'angs*, of cooking pots, of hoes, of stools, of guns—all the solid objects that are so important in a society that has so little. In the production the actors must value these things, they must treat them not as theatrical props, but as the props of their very existence. It is a world in which to have two changes of clothing is to be rich. You must show that in the way you act. It is a world in which the redistribution is not a pleasant satisfying exercise, as it might be in a European commune, but instead a simple matter of life and death. The actors must try and understand need. It is almost impossible for Westerners with so little experience of suffering to think themselves into the appalling situation of the Chinese peasant in the mid-1940s. But you must find ways of understanding that the political process the play describes guarantees much more than the

8

characters' comfort: it guarantees their actual survival. And so every stage of it, every policy, every disagreement, every celebration is crucial. Show this, and you will show the essence of *Fanshen*.

Further, try and show that *Fanshen* is an optimistic document. At the end of each scene ask the question: what political point is this scene making? And then ask, does our presentation of it do everything to make that point, or is it in places contradicting that point? You will find that once you ask these questions, a lot of fussy over-characterization will drop away and arguments about motivation will be set in perspective. Instead ask the question: is our presentation positive enough?

At some time you are bound to face the question: how do I play Chinese? This question exercised the actors and directors of our workshop for many weeks. I felt impatient about their concern. It worries me not at all that in *King Lear* I don't actually believe that the early British really looked like modern Shakespearian actors, nor do I jib at their speaking verse. Certain conventions I will accept as long as they do not patronize their subjects: so no slant eyes, no make-up, no funny mannerisms, no silly externalizing. Instead work on the principle that although a Chinese peasant is as psychologically complex as a Westerner, he has a different set of limitations. On stage people are defined by what they cannot do and say, as much as by what they can. Look through the text. See what is missing in their experience. Then see what is assumed. Hinton himself points to one simple example: nobody in the book ever questions the value of the revolution, they only question its direction. After the barbaric experiences of the past, it simply never occurs to them to question the actual fact of the fanshen.

You will see what I am saying: that the production of this play must involve you in the continual definition of your objectives and the continual asking of questions. For that reason, I was wrong to be impatient with the actors and directors, for they eventually made me see that in some small sense the production techniques must mirror the fanshen itself. Now of course that sense is limited by the fact that the actors cannot feel the necessity of a fanshen in the way the Chinese did. Their lives will not depend on it. But unless they identify with the techniques of the fanshen and use them in the production—group discussion, self-criticism and so on—then their version of the play will probably be shallow and super- ficial.

Fanshen was first performed in London by the Joint Stock Theatre Group at the ICA Terrace Theatre on 22 April 1975.

Company: Philip Donaghy
Paul Freeman
Cecily Hobbs
Roderic Leigh
Tony Mathews
Philip McGough
Pauline Melville
David Rintoul
Tony Rohr

Directed by William Gaskill and Max Stafford-Clark
Designed by Di Seymour

ACT I

Fanshen *is an accurate historical record of what once happened in one village four hundred miles south-west of Peking.*

Every revolution creates new words. The Chinese revolution created a whole new vocabulary. A most important word in this vocabulary was 'fanshen'. Literally it means 'to turn the body' or 'to turn over'. To China's hundreds of millions of landless and land-poor peasants it meant to stand up, to throw off the landlord yoke, to gain land, stock, implements and houses. But it meant much more than this. It meant to enter a new world. That is why the book is called Fanshen. *It is the story of how the peasants of Long Bow built a new world.*

This version of William Hinton's book should be played with about nine actors taking the thirty or so parts. There are no sets, and no lighting cues. It should be performed using authentic props and costumes. At one end of the acting area is a small raised platform on which certain scenes are played. The rest of the acting area thrusts forward into the audience.

SECTION ONE
When the audience are in, the actors appear one by one with a piece of information. Then they begin to work on stage at their land, or washing, or begging, or watching until they form a whole picture of the village.

CH'UNG-LAI'S WIFE: The village of Long Bow is situated four hundred miles south-west of Peking. One thousand people live there. In 1946 nearly all the people lived off the land. Landlords claimed from fifty to seventy per cent of their tenants' crop in rent. The rate of interest on loans went as

13

high as one hundred per cent every twenty days.

I am Ch'ung-lai's wife. I have no land.

CHENG-K'UAN: A family might possess a few sections of house, each section six foot by nine, made of adobe and straw. Each person might own a quilt, a quilted jacket, cotton trousers, cotton shoes. A bowl.

I am Cheng-k'uan. I have one acre.

T'IEN-MING: The soil of Long Bow was poor. Without manure nothing would grow. The main manure was human manure, the foundation of the whole economy.

I am T'ien-ming. I have half an acre.

HU HSUEH-CHEN: Chinese peasant women had their marriages arranged by their parents, and were often sold as children into landlords' households. Only when a woman became a mother-in-law in her own home did she command any power in a household. All the older women had their feet bound when they were young and could only move short distances.

I am Hu Hsueh-chen, beggar. No land.

FA-LIANG: In Long Bow landlords and rich peasants owned two acres or more per head. Middle peasants owned one acre, poor peasants half an acre per head. Hired labourers owned no land at all.

I am Fa-liang, a hired labourer.

SHEN CHING-HO: By far the largest building in Long Bow was the Catholic church, a Gothic building built in 1916 by Belgian Catholics. It acted as a bank and orphanage. Many of the poor of Long Bow bought their wives from the orphanage because it was cheaper.

I am Shen Ching-ho, a landlord. Twenty-three acres.

MAN-HSI: For thousands of years China was ruled by emperors. When the Japanese invaded most of the country was controlled by the Nationalist Party, the Kuomintang, under Chiang Kai-shek. Throughout the Japanese occupation, the most successful and only lasting resistance was organized by the Communist Eighth Route Army. By 1945 when the Japanese left, parts of China were controlled by the Nationalists and parts by the Communists. Long Bow was at the edge.

Man-hsi. Half an acre.

YU-LAI (*holding up a copy*): This is the book *Fanshen* by
William Hinton.*

I am Yu-lai, an ex-bandit.

TUI-CHIN: Literally the word 'fanshen' means to turn the body
or to turn over. This is a record of one village's life between 1945 and 1949. Many of the characters are still
alive.

(*The peasants work. The landlord on the platform watches.
Then he leaves.*

The house lights go down.)

I

(T'IEN-MING *boxes the compass with a megaphone from on top
of the church tower.*)

T'IEN-MING: There will be a meeting. There will be a meeting
today. In the square after the noon meal. There will be a
meeting.

(*The men look up from their work.*)

FA-LIANG: A meeting.

TUI-CHIN: Twenty years ago we had a meeting.

CHENG-K'UAN: About the church, about who owned the
vegetable garden.

(TUI-CHIN *shrugs and smiles.*)

TUI-CHIN: Another meeting.

(*They slowly move from work and gather in the square.
They squat down and wait till they are joined. Meanwhile the
following scene is played simultaneously.* KUO TE-YU *is being
guarded by* MAN-HSI. *He carries his rifle like a hoe with a red
tassel on the end. The scene is played on the platform.*
T'IEN-MING *comes in.*)

T'IEN-MING: A battle. Eight miles away. Outside Changchih.

MAN-HSI: Are we winning?

T'IEN-MING: Not yet.

MAN-HSI: Then we can't go ahead.

T'IEN-MING: Tie him up.

* The actor should give publisher and current price.

15

MAN-HSI: T'ien-ming.

T'IEN-MING: Tie him up. We have messages telling us the Eighth Route Army have liberated fifty million people. Three hundred thousand square miles.

MAN-HSI: But for how long?

T'IEN-MING: It doesn't matter. Elsewhere the Japanese are handing over only to the Kuomintang.

(KUO TE-YU *moans*.)

Be quiet. The Kuomintang are leaving in wartime puppet governments, puppet troops. They even have the Japanese fighting for them against us in places.

MAN-HSI: Then we must wait till we know . . .

T'IEN-MING: The Kuomintang are throwing their troops into regaining the Liberated Areas. Civil war.

MAN-HSI: If it's still going on, the people will be frightened to . . .

T'IEN-MING: What else can we do? Get that leg up.

MAN-HSI: Can't we wait? Can't we wait for victory before we begin?

T'IEN-MING: No. Above our heads?

MAN-HSI: Very good.

T'IEN-MING: Make a show.

(*They hoist the trussed* KUO TE-YU *above their heads*.)

There is a crack in history one inch wide. We fought for it and we must use it.

(*They hoist* KUO TE-YU *down from the platform. They carry him out and throw him down in front of the crowd*.)

Countrymen. Your eight years' suffering, your eight years at the hands of the Japanese are over. Their troops have gone. Now—revenge on traitors.

(*Cheers from the crowd*.)

Kuo Te-yu was head of the village for the last two years of the Japanese occupation. He was a collaborator.

PEASANTS: Kill him. Rape his mother.

T'IEN-MING: Yes. But with your help.

(MAN-HSI *stands back from the bundle*.)

T'IEN-MING: You all suffered under this man. You all know what he did. I therefore am asking you to speak it out. We

16

are asking for your help. No one has ever asked your help before. Look at him. There's nothing to fear. You can touch him. Everyone here has a grievance, everyone here has the right to accuse, we all have the same thoughts in our heads. Those of us who fought in the resistance are now asking for your help. You must be the ones to beat down traitors, you must accuse. Who will be the first to speak?

(*Silence. People move slightly away from the bundle.*)

Fa-liang, what are you thinking? Cheng-k'uan? Tui-chin, have you . . .

(*Silence.*)

Release him.

MAN-HSI: He . . .

T'IEN-MING: Untie the ropes.

(MAN-HSI *starts to undo the bundle. The people watch. Then* YU-LAI *gets up slowly.*)

YU-LAI: Why not just take him up into the hills . . .

T'IEN-MING: No . . .

YU-LAI: And do whatever you want, shoot him, it's your . . .

T'IEN-MING: He must be tried, in public, by the peasants of Long Bow, by the people he's oppressed . . .

YU-LAI: You're just afraid to kill him yourself . . .

(*They start speaking simultaneously, each riding over the other's sentences.* YU-LAI *lecturing at* T'IEN-MING.)

T'IEN-MING: No . . .

YU-LAI: Because the Kuomintang are eight miles away . . .

T'IEN-MING: I'm asking for your help . . .

YU-LAI: And if they come back . . .

T'IEN-MING: No one has ever asked anything of you before . . .

YU-LAI: Then Kuo Te-yu will be reappointed . . .

T'IEN-MING: I am asking you to speak out your memories . . .

YU-LAI: And anyone who has spoken at the meeting today . . .

T'IEN-MING: That's all, to say what we all know . . .

YU-LAI: Anyone who has taken part in the struggle . . .

T'IEN-MING: Just to speak it out.

YU-LAI: Will be shot. Tell them that.

(*Pause.*)

17

T'IEN-MING: So what are you saying?

YU-LAI: What are you saying?

T'IEN-MING: Would you prefer to live under the Kuomintang? Would you like Kuo Te-yu reappointed? Your harvest seized, your goods impounded, your friends in the resistance shot? You want to see more of your friends hanged by the hair until their scalp comes away from their skull? (*Pause.*) Then what are you saying?

YU-LAI: I'm saying . . .

T'IEN-MING: Yes?

YU-LAI: Those who accuse collaborators may themselves be killed.

T'IEN-MING: Yes. (*Pause.*) So will you speak first?
(*Pause.* YU-LAI *stuck.* T'IEN-MING *smiles.*)
Wang Yu-lai?

YU-LAI: Don't laugh at me.

T'IEN-MING: I'm not laughing.

YU-LAI: If you . . .

T'IEN-MING: Of course, if you're frightened . . .

YU-LAI: Wait. I'm thinking.
(*The villagers smile, enjoying* YU-LAI's *difficulty. Then slowly he sits down.*)
Give me time to think.
(KUO TE-YU *is now untied.* T'IEN-MING *stares hard at the crowd.*)

T'IEN-MING: The resistance worked eight years. Some of you . . . silently supported us, in secret. Now the war against the Japanese is over, a civil war may begin. If we cannot beat down the traitors . . . (*He moves towards* KUO.)
You're frightened of him. There's nothing. Look. (*He puts his finger inside* KUO's *mouth, between his teeth. Holds it there. Looks at the crowd. Takes it out.*) There's nothing there.

YU-LAI: You've paid him not to bite you.

T'IEN-MING: Come here.

YU-LAI: No.

T'IEN-MING: Come here.
(YU-LAI *looks round, then walks up.* T'IEN-MING *places him*

dead opposite KUO TE-YU.)
Was this man a collaborator?
(YU-LAI *nods*.)
Did you suffer at his hands?
(YU-LAI *nods*.)
Did he steal your harvest?
(YU-LAI *nods*.)
Did he butcher your friends?
(YU-LAI *nods*.)
Accuse him.
(*A pause. Then* YU-LAI *strikes* KUO TE-YU *across the face.
Then he smashes a fist under his jaw.* KUO TE-YU *falls back.
Then* YU-LAI *picks him up, hits him again.*)
Accuse him.
(YU-LAI *stands him unsteadily on his feet, then takes a pace
back.*)

YU-LAI: Shen So-tzu was tortured for eighteen days, starved and
shot. He was responsible. He betrayed him to the
Japanese. I saw the body. I know it happened.

T'IEN-MING: Name him.

YU-LAI: Kuo Te-yu.
(YU-LAI *goes back and takes his place in the crowd. Silence.
Then a voice from a man still sitting in the crowd.*)

CHENG-K'UAN: Kung Lai-pao was cut to pieces with a samurai
sword.

T'IEN-MING: Stand up.

CHENG-K'UAN (*stands*): It was his treachery. Kuo Te-yu.

FA-LIANG: I was made to hand over three bags of grain or told
the Japanese would burn my whole crop. He took it away
and kept it.

T'IEN-MING: Name him.

FA-LIANG: Kuo Te-yu.

TUI-CHIN: He sent me to work in the fields, I was never paid.
One day . . .
(*Then an outbreak of shouting in the crowd, all on top of each
other.*)

CHENG K'UAN: Kill the donkey's tool.

TUI-CHIN: Rape his mother.

19

MAN-HSI: Kill him.

> (*They all rush forward on* KUO TE-YU *and start a huge brawl.*
> T'IEN-MING *throws himself in to try and protect* KUO TE-YU.)

T'IEN-MING: Leave him. Leave him. He's only a puppet.

KUO TE-YU (*screaming now*): I carried orders, I was only carrying
out orders.

T'IEN-MING: Leave him.

> (*He manages to clear a space for* KUO TE-YU.)

He took orders. Let him testify.

KUO TE-YU: I was told what to do.

YU-LAI: Who told you?

KUO TE-YU: Wen Ch'i-Yun . . .

T'IEN-MING: Commander of the puppet garrison, Long Bow
fort.

KUO TE-YU: Murderer. Killed many in my sight. Shen
Chi-mei . . .

T'IEN-MING: Head of Fifth District Police . . .

KUO TE-YU: Killed many. Ordered many dead. Took prisoners.
Cut their hands, their fingers. He ran the camps.

> (*Silence.*)

TUI-CHIN: Shoot them.

T'IEN-MING: Nobody will be shot, nobody, until they have been
tried by you. You have taken their lives into your hands,
you, the peasants of Long Bow. It lies with you. Do you
understand?

2

(*The peasants gather to watch. Still figures. Two men are lined up
with sacks over their heads.*)

T'IEN-MING: Down with traitors, down with Kuomintang agents,
liquidate the bloody eight years' debt.

> (MAN-HSI *cocks his rifle.*)

Arrested, tried, found guilty by the people. Wen Ch'i-Yun,
commander of the puppet garrison, Long Bow fort. Shen
Chi-mei, head of the Fifth District Police.

> (MAN-HSI *shoots them. They fall. The people watch as* T'IEN-
> MING *and* MAN-HSI *strip the bodies of their clothes. They then
> hold the clothes out to the people.*)

Here. The fruits of struggle. What we have seized from
traitors. Take them. You have earned them. You deserve
them. You have played your part. You have condemned
the traitors, you have executed collaborators.

(*The people look at the clothes, but they turn away and will
not take them. Then* SHEN CHING-HO, *the landlord, passes
across the back of the stage. They scatter.* T'IEN-MING *and
MAN-HSI are left holding out the goods.*)

Take them. Take them.

(*There is no one left.*)

SECTION TWO

I

Slogan: **Asking Basic Questions**

SECRETARY LIU *appears, to address three cadres from Long Bow.*
T'IEN-MING, MAN-HSI *and* YU-LAI. *They sit in a square.*

Slogan: **The Visit of Secretary Liu**

LIU: An island in the centre of China. A province held by the
Eighth Route Army. Now—a short ceasefire in the war
between the Kuomintang and ourselves. During this time
the possibility of a coalition is to be explored. But for a
time our ground is safe. Our army protects us. In
Lucheng County there is a People's Government. Our duty,
the duty of all village leaders, is to consolidate the successes
of the Anti-Traitor movement. The history of China is a
history of bloody and violent rebellion. But always the
blood runs down the gutter and nothing is changed. How
are we to make sure this time, in this tight circle, the
overturning holds?

The difference is, this time, we think. We ask questions.
We analyse. This is why I have come to talk to you.
Today you must consider a single question. Who depends
upon whom for a living?

MAN-HSI: What's the answer?

LIU: No, you must think.

(T'IEN-MING *gets up and crosses to another part of the stage
where he is joined by the peasants from the previous scene:*

TUI-CHIN, CH'UNG-LAI's WIFE, HU HSUEH-CHEN, FA-LIANG.
There are now two meetings which are played antiphonally for the rest of the section.)

Slogan: **The Forming of the Peasants' Association**

T'IEN-MING: If we peasants are to organize ourselves we must know why. We must start with questions. We must find an answer to the most important question. Who depends upon whom for a living? Well can anyone . . .

MAN-HSI: We depend on the land.

LIU: On whom?

MAN-HSI: On the person who owns the land.

LIU: The landlord.

MAN-HSI: Yes. We depend on the landlord for a living.

LIU: Yu-lai?

MAN-HSI: If the landlord didn't rent us land, we'd starve.

LIU: But who gave him the land?

MAN-HSI: He bought it.

LIU: How did he make the money to buy it?

YU-LAI: If . . .

MAN-HSI: No, let me, leave this to me. It's not . . . Listen . . . I've forgotten what I was going to say.

FA-LIANG: Why do we need to know?

T'IEN-MING: You must not just do things. You must know why you do things.

FA-LIANG: Why?

T'IEN-MING: Because you need a theory . . .

TUI-CHIN: What's a theory?

MAN-HSI: The question is . . . I don't see it. Why ask it? What answer do you want? What do you want me to say?

LIU: You must work it out for yourself. If you want to serve the people you need to think.

MAN-HSI: Collaborators, yes, I could understand, should be executed; this, I don't understand.

T'IEN-MING: Fa-liang. Tell us something of your life.

FA-LIANG: My life?

T'IEN-MING: Yes. Just tell us.

FA-LIANG: I was fourteen when I went to work for Shen Ching-ho. My mother had been ill, my father had to

borrow four dollars from the landlord to buy medicine.
So to guarantee the loan he lent me to the landlord to work
for seven years. I was always hungry. Twice I was ill. But
no matter how hard I worked I couldn't begin to pay off
the debt. By the time I'd worked for him three years, we
owed him fifteen dollars instead of four. And then, after
seven years, by the time he'd taken off all the things he
claimed I'd broken, all the time I was sick, what was left
was not enough to pay even the interest on the debt. So I
had no wages at all. I had worked seven years. And he
gave me nothing. At the end I tore down two sections of
our house, I tore out the timbers. And only then could I
pay back the original debt.

CH'UNG-LAI'S WIFE: I was sold at the age of nine to be
Ch'ung-lai's wife. I then had to serve in his family for six
years before I married him. I was a child wife, everyone
beat me. One day my mother-in-law broke my arm. The
water in the pot was boiling. I asked her what I should
cook in it. She didn't answer. I asked her again. She
picked up an iron poker and broke my arm with it. She
said I annoyed her. I lay on the k'ang for a fortnight,
couldn't work or move. Then Ch'ung-lai's family threw
me out. Ch'ung-lai went to Taiyuan to get work pulling a
rickshaw, I went to work as a cook for a landlord. After
about six years we earned enough to buy one acre of land,
but it only yielded two bags of grain. After we had paid
taxes, there was nothing left.

LIU: Why should one man have the right to say 'This land is
mine' and then without doing any work himself demand
half of what's grown on it?

MAN-HSI: He owns it. It's his, he can do what he likes.

LIU: Is it right?

MAN-HSI: Listen. I work for a landlord. He feeds me. At the
end of the year he pays me. If he had cheated me, then I
could . . . discuss it with you. But as he doesn't . . . then
. . . so.

LIU: So tell me. Who depends on whom?

MAN-HSI: It's . . .

23

YU-LAI: I . . .

MAN-HSI: Say the thing again.

LIU: Who depends on whom?

T'IEN-MING: Hsueh-chen.

HSUEH-CHEN: My father was a labourer but he sold me to a
husband against my will. My husband could find no work,
could barely live. So he gambled what money we had. We
lost our only quilt, we were left with nothing. I've had
three children. One I saw the Japanese kill, a soldier with
his boot, then with his sword. The second died of worms
crawling out of him. So I threw my husband out of the
house, took my third child, begged alone. People give me
nothing. I live in the fields, eat herbs, sleep in the straw.
And my third child is alive.

MAN-HSI: There has to be somebody to give us work to do.

YU-LAI: Why?

MAN-HSI: If there were no landlords we'd starve.

TUI-CHIN: I once went to my landlord to ask for more wages.
He said, if you're poor it's because the heavens will it, it's
because your grave is poorly located. All you can do is
wait for your luck to change. Select a more suitable spot
for your own grave and hope that the eight ideographs of
earth and heaven are in better conjunction when your son
is born.

T'IEN-MING: What do you conclude?

Slogan: **They Talked For Eight Hours**

T'IEN-MING: We have all suffered. But we've never asked why.
If we had to suffer. Do you see?

MAN-HSI: I don't understand.

Slogan: **They Talked For Three Days**

T'IEN-MING: Think. All think of your lives. Think what you've
endured, what have you suffered for?

YU-LAI: What can they do which we can't? Nothing. What can
we do which they can't? We can work. Our labour
transforms their land. We make it valuable, we create
their wealth.

CH'UNG-LAI'S WIFE: We have all suffered for them.

T'IEN-MING: So who depends on whom?

24

YU-LAI: We make them rich, they depend on our labour, they depend on us.

[CH'UNG-LAI'S WIFE: They depend on us.

[T'IEN-MING: Yes.

[LIU: Yes.

[FA-LIANG: They depend on us.

[YU-LAI: Take us away, they'd die. Take them away, we live.

[T'IEN-MING: You do not depend on them. They depend on you. Understand this and everything you have ever known is changed.

LIU: We have liberated a peach tree heavy with fruit. Who is to be allowed to pick the fruit? Those who have tended and watered the tree? Or those who have sat at the side of the orchard with folded arms?

YU-LAI: We shouldn't even pay rent.

Slogan: **They Stopped Paying Rent**

LIU: The policy in the Liberated Areas is to ask simply for a reduction in rents and interest charges. But here in Lucheng County, you—the leaders—will go ahead of the policy.

(*They shake hands with* LIU *and say good-bye. Then join the peasants.*)

T'IEN-MING: Now surely we can right the wrongs of the past. Already in many places the landlords have been beaten down. We have only to follow the example of others. Then we can all fanshen.

(*Above the platform they raise a red banner saying* FANSHEN.)

SECTION THREE

I

Slogan: **Settling Accounts**

At one end CH'UNG-WANG *sits with a pair of scales, ready to receive rent. At the other on the platform* CHING-HO *sits, his finger-nails being tended by his* DAUGHTER.

CHING-HO: Shen Ching-ho. A landlord.

CH'UNG-WANG: Kuo Ch'ung-wang. A landlord.

(A group of peasants form outside CH'UNG-WANG's *house. Then* TUI-CHIN *steps from the group and into the house.)*

CH'UNG-WANG: Rent.

TUI-CHIN: The peasants have decided to stop paying rent.

CH'UNG-WANG: Come here.

TUI-CHIN: We have decided it's wrong to pay rent. And we have decided you took too much in the past . . .

CH'UNG-WANG: Come here.

TUI-CHIN: Through the war, you charged us too much. And we want it back.

CH'UNG-WANG: Tui-chin, the land you farm . . .

TUI-CHIN: Also interest on loans, that was too high . . .

CH'UNG-WANG: You have just lost.

TUI-CHIN: And we want that back. Any land you seized when we couldn't pay our debts . . .

CH'UNG-WANG: The house you live in . . .

TUI-CHIN: We want that back. Also there are to be penalties for when you hit us . . .

CH'UNG-WANG: You have just lost.

TUI-CHIN: Or abused us or starved us . . .

CH'UNG-WANG: The clothes you are wearing . . .

TUI-CHIN: If it's wrong to pay rent . . .

CH'UNG-WANG: You have just lost.

TUI-CHIN: It must always have been wrong.

CH'UNG-WANG: Come here.

*(*CH'UNG-WANG *rises to strike* TUI-CHIN. *At once the villagers invade the house.)*

CHENG-K'UAN: Elected Chairman, Peasants' Association.

YU-LAI: Elected Vice-Chairman, Peasants' Association. Find his grain.

CH'UNG-WANG: Peasants' Association?

*(*FA-LIANG *goes out to search for his grain.)*

YU-LAI: You are to attend a meeting at which your past life will be reviewed. Everything you have taken from us unfairly since the war began—rent, interest, land—you will return. Everything you have done to us since the Japanese came you will pay for. In one day we will add up the bill for your life.

26

FA-LIANG: Look.

YU-LAI: Until then we are seizing your grain as security for your debt. And we are posting militia on your land. (FA-LIANG *returns, throwing down a rotten bag of mildewed grain.*)

FA-LIANG: Look. Look.

TUI-CHIN: It's rotten. Why? Why did you let it go rotten? How could you?

FA-LIANG: This was salt.

TUI-CHIN: Salt. This was salt. (*He takes the jar and flings the contents in* CH'UNG-WANG'*s face. It has hydrolized.*) One year when I couldn't pay my rent you took my whole harvest. Now I find it's in here rotting. Why?

YU-LAI: He was hoarding it. He was hoping to make money.

FA-LIANG: People died . . .

YU-LAI: Wait . . .

TUI-CHIN: Le-Miao starved to death on your land . . .

YU-LAI: Wait . . .

TUI-CHIN: All the time this was here.

FA-LIANG: Once I came begging, I crawled for grain . . .

YU-LAI: Wait . . .

TUI-CHIN: Kill him. Cut off his hands.

YU-LAI: Wait. Wait for the meeting.

Slogan: **Fifty-eight Accusations**
       (*The group re-form. The other villagers go, leaving just* FA-LIANG, TUI-CHIN, CHENG-K'UAN *and* YU-LAI *facing* CH'UNG-WANG.)

YU-LAI: The people have accused you. Now you must pay.

FA-LIANG: There are six good bags of grain. That's all I can find.

CHENG-K'UAN: It's not enough.

TUI-CHIN: We've measured his land. Thirteen acres.

CHENG-K'UAN: Not enough.

YU-LAI: He owes the village one hundred bags of grain. It's his blood debt. And his sweat debt. He must settle accounts.

CHENG-K'UAN: Look. Here is a list of everything you took from us. Where is it?

CH'UNG-WANG: I don't know.

27

FA-LIANG: You turned it into coins.

CH'UNG-WANG: I don't have any coins.

FA-LIANG: All your houses, all your stock, all your grain, your clothes are not enough to settle your account. Where are your coins?

CH'UNG-WANG: No coins.

FA-LIANG: Where are they?

(YU-LAI *clears a space. He hits* CH'UNG-WANG *twice.*)

CH'UNG-WANG: Fifty dollars. In the stove.

YU-LAI: Fa-liang. Stove.

(FA-LIANG *goes off.* YU-LAI *nods at* CHENG-K'UAN.)

YU-LAI: Cheng-k'uan.

(CHENG-K'UAN *moves round for his turn. Hits* CH'UNG-WANG.)

CH'UNG-WANG: Forty dollars.

CHENG-K'UAN: Where?

CH'UNG-WANG: Back yard.

YU-LAI: Fa-liang. Back yard.

(YU-LAI *nods now at* TUI-CHIN *who takes his turn at hitting* CH'UNG-WANG.)

CH'UNG-WANG: Thirty. Under the stable.

YU-LAI: Fa-liang. Stable. (*He turns and smiles at* TUI-CHIN.) All right?

TUI-CHIN: Yes.

YU-LAI: May we leave it to you?

TUI-CHIN: Of course.

YU-LAI: It may be slow.

CHENG-K'UAN: Good night.

YU-LAI: Good night.

(*They smile and go off.* TUI-CHIN *looks at* CH'UNG-WANG, *then kicks him again.* SHEN CHING-HO *rises.*)

CH'UNG-WANG: Another fifteen. Under the tree.

TUI-CHIN: Fa-liang. Tree.

(*On the platform* CHING-HO *suddenly speaks.*)

CHING-HO: My oldest clothes. (*He changes and dirties his hands.*) One bag of white flour.

(*His* DAUGHTER *fetches it. He turns to her.*) Kiss me.

(*She does so. Then they set off across the village.* FA-LIANG

28

returns with the coins.)

TUI-CHIN: Did you get them?

FA-LIANG: Yes.

(*They look at each other.*)

TUI-CHIN: When I was born my family wanted to celebrate. But they had to borrow money for dumplings. And so before I could speak, I was already in debt to the landlord.

A man stands up to his neck in water, so that even a ripple is enough to drown him.

(*The scene scatters, as* CHING-HO *stops at the door of* YU-LAI *and* CHENG-K'UAN *who are sitting at home. He puts the bag down and gestures to his* DAUGHTER *to stay outside, unseen. Then he goes in.*)

CHING-HO: New Year.

YU-LAI: Yes.

CHING-HO: I had to come.

(*He smiles.* YU-LAI *looks at* CHENG-K'UAN.)

A new life. Just to say a Happy New Year, a happy new life.

YU-LAI: Yes.

CHING-HO: That's good. Thank you. (*He goes to the door, slips his hand out, brings in the bag.*) I know your life is hard. On this soil. The valuable work you are doing. Service to the community. But we are all . . . citizens of one village. Please no ceremony but . . . help yourselves to the flour and pass a happy New Year. (*He puts the bag down and walks backwards away.*) If at any time you should meet any difficulty in your new life in any way you should know my door is as it has always been, open, and I am as I have always been, ready to help. (*He gestures his* DAUGHTER *in.*) This is my daughter. She has always wanted to . . . (*Silence.*)

Yours. Good night. (*He goes out.*)

(YU-LAI *and* CHENG-K'UAN *look at each other. The* DAUGHTER *stands silent, dignified, ignored for the rest of the scene.*)

YU-LAI: What does he take us for? Rats who can be bought for one bag of flour? One bag? I'm worth a thousand bags. I am a granary.

(CHENG-K'UAN *looks at the impassive girl, then goes over to the flour, puts a finger in, licks it, then stares in the bag as down a deep well.*)

The richest landlord in Long Bow. In the famine year he gave us nothing, now suddenly we all belong to one village. And we are offered flour.

(T'IEN MING *appears on the platform.*)

T'IEN MING: Never trust a landlord, never protect a landlord. There is only one road and that is to struggle against them.

(*A banner descends reading:* **Never Trust A Landlord, Never Protect A Landlord, There Is Only One Road And That Is To Struggle Against Them**)

2

(CHING-HO *is seized as he goes home, stripped, tortured. Silent tableaux of the scene as it is described.*)

MAN-HSI: When the final struggle began Ching-ho was faced with accusations from more than half the village. Old women who had never spoken in public before stood up to accuse him. Altogether one hundred and eighty people testified. Ching-ho had no answer to any of them. When the Association met to decide what he owed, it came to four hundred bags of grain.

CHENG-K'UAN: That evening all the people went to Ching-ho's courtyard to help take over his property. It was very cold. We built bonfires and the flames shot up towards the stars. It was very beautiful.

YU-LAI: We dug up all his money, beating him, digging, finding more, beating him, digging, finding more. By the time the sun was rising in the sky we had five hundred dollars.

T'IEN-MING: We were all tired and hungry. We decided to eat all the things Ching-ho had prepared for the New Year. There was a whole crock full of dumplings stuffed with pork and peppers. We even had shrimp. Everyone ate their fill and didn't notice the cold.

SHEN CHING-HO: Of the seven landlords in Long Bow, three
    died after being beaten to death by the Peasants' Associa-
    tion. Two more died of starvation when they had been
    driven from their land. Shen Ching-ho was luckier: he
    ran away and became a teacher in a primary school.

3
Slogan: **Distribution Of Fruits**
(YU-LAI *speaks from on high.* T'IEN-MING *stands beside him.* CHENG-
K'UAN *organizes the peasants while* MAN-HSI *counts with an abacus.*)
YU-LAI: We have seized the wealth from fifteen families. Two
    hundred and eighty-six acres of land, twenty-six draft
    animals, four hundred sections of house. And behind the
    temple doors: everything they own.
    (*The peasants stand in single file while* CHENG-K'UAN
    explains.)
CHENG-K'UAN: You'll be given a number.
FA-LIANG: Yes.
CHENG-K'UAN: The number will be the number of pounds of
    grain you've been allocated.
FA-LIANG: Yes.
CHENG-K'UAN: You may then either keep the grain or change it
    into any object you want from inside the temple. Each
    object has its price marked on it. A plough I think three
    hundredweight of grain. A shovel fifty pounds, a slipper
    two, a rattle one, so on.
MAN-HSI: A hundred and eighty.
CHENG-K'UAN: You may spend a hundred and eighty pounds
    of grain.
YU-LAI (*from above*): The poorest allowed in first.
CHENG-K'UAN: Ch'ou-har. Because you are poor and have many
    needs, we have put your number up.
MAN-HSI: A hundred and ninety.
CHENG-K'UAN: You may spend a hundred and ninety pounds
    of grain.
CH'OU-HAR: A hundred and ninety.
CHENG-K'UAN: Hsueh-chen. Your number is not as high as
    others. There are only two in your family. We know you

31

suffered a great deal but you did not speak at meetings.
You did not speak out your grievances at landlords.
(*She nods, too shy to reply.*)

CHENG-K'UAN: How can we know unless you speak out?
Anyway you've got what you need.

MAN-HSI: One hundred and twenty.

CHENG-K'UAN: You may spend one hundred and twenty pounds
of grain. Go in. Next.

TUI-CHIN: Tui-chin.

CHENG-K'UAN: Yes. Now, you have denounced many landlords.
You have been active in the struggle from the start, spoken
at meetings. This should ensure you a lot. But in every
case we have also balanced people's grievances against their
needs. And you are a single man, who has a lot of the
implements he needs. So your number has come down.

TUI-CHIN: What if I want a cow, but haven't been given
enough grain?

CHENG-K'UAN: Then you'll get a share in a cow.

TUI-CHIN: A share?

T'IEN-MING: Yes. Why not?

TUI-CHIN: Share a cow?

T'IEN-MING: Four families, one leg each.

TUI-CHIN: Very good.

MAN-HSI: A hundred and fifty pounds of grain.

CHENG-K'UAN: Next.

CH'UNG-LAI'S WIFE: I am Ch'ung-lai's wife.

CHENG-K'UAN: Yes, yes I know. Many—grievances—yes—and
also great need. Both. Grievances and need both high.
Man-hsi?
(*Pause.*)

CH'UNG-LAI'S WIFE: What do you get?

CHENG-K'UAN: What?

CH'UNG-LAI'S WIFE: The leaders, what do the leaders get? You,
the Chairman of the Association. Yu-lai over there,
T'ien-ming, village head. What do you get?

T'IEN-MING: The leaders get less.

CH'UNG-LAI'S WIFE: They get some?

T'IEN-MING: They get some but they get less.

32

(YU-LAI *has been listening to this last exchange.*)

MAN-HSI: Two hundred and ten.

CHENG-K'UAN: Go into the temple. Make your choice.

CH'UNG-LAI'S WIFE: Thank you. Thank you. (*She goes in.*)

(YU-LAI, CHENG-K'UAN *and* T'IEN-MING *are left outside.*)

YU-LAI: Why?

CHENG-K'UAN: Mm?

YU-LAI: Why less?

CHENG-K'UAN: Less because . . .

T'IEN-MING: Less because you're the leaders and you must wait for the peasants to suggest you get some.

YU-LAI: Wait for them?

T'IEN-MING: Yes.

YU-LAI: Well it's not worth it. I'd be better off as a peasant.

T'IEN-MING: Yes.

(*Pause.*)

YU-LAI: I think we should get something. Not for ourselves, more for expenses, for the Association. If we took over the inn, managed it, that would help pay for the school, pay for the oil we need for lamps for Association meetings. We're going to have to make some money somehow.

CHENG-K'UAN: Take over the inn?

YU-LAI: Why not?

(*Pause.*)

CHENG-K'UAN: Put it to the people.

YU-LAI: I thought we were waiting for them to put it to us.

(*They smile.*)

CHENG-K'UAN: Take over the inn.

(*The peasants begin to come out carrying loot. Some have bags of grain, some implements.* FA-LIANG *is wearing a landlord's coat.*)

HSUEH-CHEN: A quilt! A landlord's quilt!

(TUI-CHIN *comes out with a pot bigger than himself.*)

T'IEN-MING: Are you sure that's what you want?

TUI-CHIN: Certain. I've always wanted it.

FA-LIANG: All my life I have been oppressed and exploited.

TUI-CHIN: For all the grain I'm going to have.

(*He embraces* T'IEN-MING *crying.* CH'OU-HAR *has a huge bag of grain.*)

CH'OU-HAR: The bad life. The unbearable life of working for others.

CH'UNG-LAI'S WIFE: We are moving from hell to heaven. To live in your own house, to eat out of your own bowl, is the happiest life.

(YU-LAI *looks at* T'IEN-MING *and smiles.*)

SECTION FOUR

I

Night. T'IEN-MING *and* MAN-HSI *walk up and down in silence, guarding the road to Changchih.* T'IEN-MING *choosing his moment.*
Slogan: **The Party**

T'IEN-MING: Comrade. What do you think of the Eighth Route Army?

MAN-HSI: What do I think of it?
(*Silence.*)
What can I think? I used to have nothing, now I've fanshened. Everything I have the Eighth Route Army gave me.

T'IEN-MING: And the Communist Party?

MAN-HSI: Isn't that the same thing?

T'IEN-MING: Not exactly. The Party organized the army, in the army there are Party members. The Party directs the army, but most of the soldiers aren't in the Party. And it's the Party which led the battle against the landlords.

MAN-HSI: I see. (*He doesn't.*) Where is the Party then, where can you find it?

T'IEN-MING: I . . .

MAN-HSI: Do you know?

T'IEN-MING: Yes.

MAN-HSI: Well?

T'IEN-MING: It's many miles away, some hundreds of miles. In the countryside. Would you come with me?

MAN-HSI: Of course. Let's go. Let's go tomorrow.

T'IEN-MING: It's a long way. And through Kuomintang country. It's difficult. Dangerous.

34

MAN-HSI: It doesn't matter, you say the Party led us to fanshen, so we must find it, let's go.

T'IEN-MING: Don't rush into it. You . . .

MAN-HSI: Go on.

T'IEN-MING: You may be risking your life.

MAN-HSI: Well?

T'IEN-MING: You may be risking your family's life.

MAN-HSI: I've made up my mind.

T'IEN-MING: Man-hsi . . .

MAN-HSI: Why do you talk about danger as if we weren't in danger already?

T'IEN-MING: In that case . . . your journey is over. The Party is here. I am a member of the Communist Party.
(*Silence.*)

MAN-HSI: Why did you trick me?

T'IEN-MING: Because the Communist Party is an illegal organization.

MAN-HSI: So?

T'IEN-MING: If the enemy returns we will all be killed. Membership is secret. Even if you are arrested and beaten to death, you must never admit you belong.

MAN-HSI: You deceived me.

T'IEN-MING: Listen . . .

MAN-HSI: Who else in Long Bow?

T'IEN-MING: You'd be the first.
(*Pause.*)

MAN-HSI: What do you hope to do? To take over the village?

T'IEN-MING: Never.

MAN-HSI: What then?

T'IEN-MING: The Party must be the backbone of the village. It must educate, study, persuade, build up the People's organizations—the Peasants' Association, the Village Government, the Women's Association, the People's Militia, it must co-ordinate all these, give them a clear line to follow, a policy that will unite everyone who can be united. Without the Party the village is a bowl of loose sand. So its members must get up earlier, work harder, attend more meetings, stay up later than anyone else,

35

worry before anyone else is worried. We must become the
best organized, the most serious group in the village. All
in secret. We must lead, not by force but by example. By
being good people. By being good Communists.
(*Pause.*)

MAN-HSI: I'd hoped for something . . .

T'IEN-MING: Yes.
(*Pause.*)
Do you see? Do you see how hard it is? And how far? And
how dangerous?

2

(*In a series of tableaux on the platform* HU HSUEH-CHEN, *her husband
and* T'IEN-MING *act out the story that* CH'UNG-LAI's WIFE *tells.*)

CH'UNG-LAI's WIFE: Liberation and the settling accounts
movement were to Hu Hsueh-chen what water is to a
parched desert. She won clothes and threw away her rags,
she won a quilt and threw away her flea-infested straw,
she won land and gave up begging. Knowing that these
gains were the result of struggle and not gifts from heaven,
she attended every meeting and supported those who were
active although she herself was afraid to speak in public.
Then she met a revolutionary cadre who helped to make
her fanshen complete. This man, a doctor, asked for her
hand in marriage. She hesitated. She asked for a conference to tell him the whole story of her life. She told him
she could not stand any more suffering or oppression at the
hands of a man. He persuaded Hu Hsueh-chen that he
was a man of principle, and that, most important, as a
product of the revolutionary army and its Communist
education, he believed in equality for women.
They were married in February 1946. Her husband began
even to cook his own supper so his wife could attend
meetings—something unheard of in Long Bow. She
became more active when he explained that fanshen could
only be achieved through struggle. She finally mastered
her shyness and became secretary of the Women's
Association.

36

In late 1946 her husband had to move away. He wrote her letters urging her to work hard. 'When you run into trouble, don't be gloomy. For there can be no trouble to compare with the past.' One day Man-hsi came to talk to her about the Communist Party. Then later T'ien-ming came and asked her if anyone had spoken to her on the subject. She knew the Party was meant to be secret so she denied having been approached.

A few days later T'ien-ming came back with an application form and helped her fill it out. He asked if she would give her life for the Party.

HSUEH-CHEN: I would.

CH'UNG-LAI'S WIFE: And he enrolled her in the Party to which her husband, unknown to her, had long belonged.

SECTION FIVE
I
Slogan: **The End of Ceasefire**
A tableau of MAN-HSI *being sent to war. He stands at the centre.*

YU-LAI:

Glorious are those who volunteer

To throw down tyrants

March to the border when the millet sprouts

Fight for the people

Defend our homes and lands

Most glorious are the volunteers.

(MAN-HSI *goes to war. The village disperse leaving* YU-LAI *with* CHENG-K'UAN. HSIEN-E *is working in the house behind.*)

Slogan: **Civil War**

YU-LAI: What's wrong?

CHENG-K'UAN: Nothing.

YU-LAI: Don't look so sad, he's happy to go. He's been given land, and we'll farm it for him while he's away.

CHENG-K'UAN: Yes.

YU-LAI: Slut. Some soup. That's why we're going to win. Because our volunteers don't have to worry about their homes.

CHENG-K'UAN: The Kuomintang . . .

YU-LAI (*turning away*): If we can keep things on the move.

(HSIEN-E *serves the soup.* T'IEN-MING *appears.*)

T'IEN-MING: There's a new directive . . .

YU-LAI: Good.

T'IEN-MING: From the Party.

CHENG-K'UAN: What does it say?

T'IEN-MING: It says if the war is to be won, the peasants must be mobilized. They must take over the land to win food to eat, clothes to wear, houses to live in. It says many peasants have still not fanshened.

YU-LAI: It's true . . .

T'IEN-MING: Serious feudal exploitation still exists.

YU-LAI: There are hundreds in the village who still don't have enough to make a living.

CHENG-K'UAN: How's it to be done?

T'IEN-MING: The land must be further redistributed.

CHENG-K'UAN: What land?

YU-LAI: We've scarcely begun. More soup.

CHENG-K'UAN: There aren't many gentry left in Long Bow. Two landlords, four rich peasants, it's not going to go very far.

YU-LAI: Middle peasants.

CHENG-K'UAN: You can start on the middle peasants certainly . . .

YU-LAI: Plenty of those . . .

CHENG-K'UAN: But if you take away their goods all you do is drive them over to the enemy side.

YU-LAI: That's a risk . . .

CHENG-K'UAN: The middle peasants already don't work as hard as they should, because if they work hard they become rich peasants, and if they become rich peasants we take it all away. Like cutting chives.

YU-LAI: Does that matter?

CHENG-K'UAN: So the people in the village who can actually make a living, who can look after themselves, who ought to be our strength, will drift over to the Kuomintang.

YU-LAI: So what do you think we should do?

(*He strikes* HSIEN-E *who has returned with more soup.*)

38

You're an idle cunt.
(*She goes.*)
The whole village is convinced the Kuomintang will
return. The Catholics openly plot our assassination,
peasants have begun to creep back in the night to return
the goods that were seized from landlords, grenades go off
in the hillside, you ask about fanshen, people have never
heard the word. We're at war. What do you think we
should do?
(*Silence.*)
Leadership. Strong leadership, Cheng-k'uan. We must keep
things moving.

CHENG-K'UAN: Well . . . (*A pause.*) What does the directive say?

T'IEN-MING: Cut off feudal tails. This time we must examine
family history. Anyone whose father or grandfather
exploited labour at any time in the past will have their
wealth confiscated.

YU-LAI: Very good.

T'IEN-MING: We must go right back, right through the last
three generations to look for any remaining trace of feudal
exploitation.

YU-LAI: Very good.

T'IEN-MING: Cheng-k'uan?
(*They look at* CHENG-K'UAN. *Then* YU-LAI *goes up to him.*)

YU-LAI: If you don't beat down the drowning dog, he jumps
up and bites your hand. (*Then he smiles and calls into the
house.*) Slut. My Luger.
(HSIEN-E *brings him his gun.*)

YU-LAI: And to work.

2

T'IEN-MING: The public meetings began again. All the
remaining members of families already under attack had
their last wealth seized. And families with any history of
exploitation were added to the list. With the enemy troops
so close and counter-revolution so likely, the campaign was
emotional and violent. When there was no more land to be
had, we ripped open ancestral tombs, leaving gaping holes

in the countryside. It looked as if the country had been bombarded with shells.

YU-LAI: But it was the living who bore the brunt of the attack. The gentry wives astonished us with their contempt for pain. We heated iron bars in the fire, but burning flesh held no terror for the women. They would die rather than tell you where their gold was hidden. They would only weaken, if at all, when their children were threatened.

CHENG-K'UAN: Slowly the advance of the Kuomintang was being halted. The military threat disappeared. And the campaign to find new wealth faded, a source of bitter disappointment to those of us who manned it. For when all the fruits had been divided, there were still many families who felt they had not fanshened.

3

(HU HSUEH-CHEN *lying on the platform, her four-year-old daughter beside her.* T'IEN-MING *at the door carrying his possessions.*)

T'IEN-MING: Hsueh-chen. Hsueh-chen.

(*She wakes.*)

I'm leaving tonight. Uh. Quiet, let me go quietly. I've been ordered to go and work at County Headquarters. You must elect a new secretary to the Party in Long Bow.

(*Silence.*)

Say nothing. I know what you're thinking. I can't help. One person doesn't make any difference. Hsueh-chen. I . . . two years ago I couldn't get a sentence out. The people . . . victory lies with the people.

(*Silence.*)

Good night. (*He goes.*)

SECTION SIX

I

Slogan: **Nineteen Forty-eight**

A single man working in the field. As at the opening of SECTION ONE.

CHENG-K'UAN *on the tower*.

CHENG-K'UAN: There will be a meeting. There will be a

meeting tonight.

(OLD TUI-CHIN *stops and looks up.*)

TUI-CHIN: Another meeting. Do the meetings never stop?

CHENG-K'UAN: Everyone to attend.

TUI-CHIN: 'Under the Nationalists too many taxes. Under the Communists, too many meetings.'

(*He picks up an enormous pile of stubble, twice his own size and starts humping it home. He pauses.* YU-LAI *sees him.*)

YU-LAI: Why aren't you at the meeting?

TUI-CHIN: They can meet without me tonight.

YU-LAI: Why?

TUI-CHIN: I'm busy. I'm tired.

YU-LAI: Come to the meeting.

TUI-CHIN: There's no point, there's nothing left to dig up, there's nothing. We'll just sit about and discuss redistributing our farts.

YU-LAI: Come to the meeting.

TUI-CHIN: Listen, we all struggled for this land. Now we're not given time to work it because we're at meetings talking about where to find more land which even if we found it we wouldn't have time to farm because we're always at meetings.

YU-LAI: Come to the meeting.

TUI-CHIN: I haven't eaten.

YU-LAI: The meeting is for your own good. (*He hits him across the face.*) It's in your interest. (*He hits him again.*) You think I don't have my work cut out without chasing up idle cunts like you?

(TUI-CHIN *stumbles away.*)

Where do you think your fanshen came from, you lazy turd?

2

(*The work team.* HOU, LITTLE LI, CH'I-YUN, CHANG CH'UER. *Platform.*)

Slogan: **The Arrival Of The Work Team**

CH'I-YUN: We paused for a moment to look down into the valley. A long flat plain, in the centre a complex of adobe

41

walls under a canopy of trees, the yellow fields stretching away on all sides. In the semi-darkness we could just see the last actions of the day: a donkey straining at a plough, a man raking corn stubble, a barefoot boy spreading night soil, a child playing with some sticks in a ditch. Over our heads the warm, motionless air hummed and whistled as a flight of swallows swooped low. The four of us stood a moment, none of us knowing each other, none of us knowing what to say. Then we began our descent into Long Bow.

(*The work team enter the village.*)

YU-LAI (*off*): You. Get out of that ditch and get to the meeting. (*Off.*) Is everyone in?

CHENG-K'UAN (*off*): All at the meeting.

(YU-LAI *appears, a broad smile on his face.*)

YU-LAI: Perhaps we should lock the doors.

(*He looks up and sees the four of them standing looking at him.*)

I don't know you.

CHI'-YUN: Comrade.

HOU: I'm Hou Pao-pei, leader of the work team. We've been sent by the government to supervise land reform in Long Bow.

YU-LAI: I see. Wang Yu-lai, Vice-Chairman Peasants' Association.

HOU: Ch'i-Yun. Chang Ch'uer. Magistrate Li. Members of the work team.

YU-LAI: Welcome to Long Bow. (*Pause.*) We are all at a meeting, you've chosen a bad time.

LITTLE LI: Is there somewhere for us to stay?

YU-LAI: I'm sure.

HOU: We will be starting work at once.

YU-LAI: Yes?

HOU: Talking to the people, finding out how they've prospered . . .

CHANG CH'UER: Agricultural methods.

HOU: Yes.

CHANG CH'UER: Mutual aid schemes.

42

HOU: Examining the progress of the movement. Elsewhere there have been shortcomings. Some landlords, rich peasants, riffraff, have sneaked into the people's organizations, where they abuse their power, ride roughshod over the people and destroy the faith of the masses in their new organizations.

YU-LAI: You can sleep in the temple. I must go to the meeting. Mutual aid scheme. Discussion. You know.

(*He looks at them, goes out. The four of them left standing.*)

HOU: Good, excellent, very good. Right.

LITTLE LI: Do you . . .

HOU: Li, can you try and find the temple? We must know where we're going to sleep. (*He laughs.*)

LITTLE LI: Yes, of course.

HOU: Chang Ch'uer, perhaps you could help, Ch'i-Yun and I will go and . . . find the meeting. Is that best?

CHANG CH'UER: I think so.

LITTLE LI: Yes.

HOU: Good, then tomorrow we start meeting the people of the village. There's a lot to be done. Good luck.

(*They scatter.* CHANG CH'UER *remains.*)

CHANG CH'UER: The first day we watched each other, the four of us, unknown to each other, scrutinizing every reaction. The second day . . .

3

(*A man with a white scarf tied round his face runs on and strangles* CHANG CH'UER. *They struggle for a long time. The man stuffs a towel down his mouth, then catches sight of* LAI-TZU *who is watching, a passer-by who happens to have caught the incident.*

The man runs off.

HU HSUEH-CHEN *runs out into the street.* HOU *appears.*)

HOU: What's happened?

HSUEH-CHEN: This man . . .

HOU: It's Chang Ch'uer.

HSUEH-CHEN: Has been attacked.

HOU: Get a doctor.

LAI-TZU: It . . .

HSUEH-CHEN: There's no doctor in the village.

HOU: Where's the nearest?

LAI-TZU: Lucheng.

HOU: What's your name? Can you carry him to Lucheng?

LAI-TZU: I can find a stretcher. (*He goes out.*)

HOU: His pulse is very weak.

HSUEH-CHEN: Who is he?

HOU: He's a member of the work team. What's this?

HSUEH-CHEN: It's a towel.

HOU: It says ger oo de morenin. 'Good morning' in English.
(LAI-TZU *returns with the stretcher.*)

LAI-TZU: I heard the attack being plotted. A few hours ago. I
know who did it.
(LITTLE LI *and* CH'I-YUN *arrive.*)

HOU: Chang Ch'uer has been attacked.

CH'I-YUN: Is it the Kuomintang?

LAI-TZU: I overheard the planning.

HOU: Lift him carefully.

LAI-TZU: It was Wang Yu-lai.

HOU: Be careful. You're hurting him.

LITTLE LI: Yu-lai?

LAI-TZU: I overheard Yu-lai talking to his friends. I was
listening . . .

LITTLE LI: Then why didn't you tell us?

HOU: Concentrate.
(*They lift the body on to the stretcher.*)

HOU: There.

LAI-TZU: Don't you want to know who did it?

HOU: I've heard what you say. Take him to Lucheng.

LAI-TZU: Do I get millet tickets?

HOU: Take him.

LAI-TZU: It's eight miles.

HOU: Little Li. Find someone who will take him.
(LITTLE LI *and* LAI-TZU *go off,* LAI-TZU *whining into the
distance.*)

LAI-TZU: I'll take him, it just is a very long way, and if he
were a wounded soldier, I'd be entitled to millet tickets,
and I just want to know if the same thing applies to . . .

44

HOU: Is he trustworthy?

HSUEH-CHEN: No. He's a Catholic.

(*A pause.* HOU *screws the towel up.* CHENG-K'UAN *arrives.*)

Hu Hsueh-chen, I'm secretary of the Women's Association.

CHENG-K'UAN: Cheng k'uan, chairman of the Peasants' Association.

HOU: You're both members of the Party, I know. Comrade Hou Pao-pei, leader of the work team.

HSUEH-CHEN: Welcome.

HOU: The man he accused . . .

HSUEH-CHEN: Yes . . .

HOU: Is a cadre in the Peasants' Association.

HSUEH-CHEN: He's Vice-Chairman.

HOU: Yes.

CHENG-K'UAN: And his son Wen-te is the head of Police.
(*Pause.*)

HSUEH-CHEN: The towels are made by a co-operative in Hantan.

HOU: These?

HSUEH-CHEN: I've seen them in Yu-lai's home.

(LITTLE LI *returns.*)

LITTLE LI: The first day we arrive . . .

CH'I-YUN: Comrade.

HOU: Give me time to think. Just give me a moment.

LITTLE LI: If the leaders of the village take to attacking the work team . . .

HOU: Please. (*He turns to* HSUEH-CHEN.) Comrades. I am a peasant like you, I come from a village, not that many miles from here. I've lived the same life, so I think you'll understand what I do.

HSUEH-CHEN: Comrade.

LITTLE LI: I think we should . . .

HOU: Just . . . let me speak. I've only been here a few hours but already the work team has heard a good deal of complaint. Some people who feel that fanshen is not complete. Some who feel they got too little, others who feel that the cadres took most. Whether this is true . . . an attack is made on the life of a member of the work team by a leader of the village on the first day we arrive to

45

investigate.

(*Pause.*)

The Vice-Chairman of the Peasants' Association must be taken to jail. His son, Wen-te, the Head of Police, will be taken to jail. His closest friends must be arrested and taken to jail. The work team will be issued with guns. All village leaders are temporarily suspended. The Women's Association. The militia suspended. The village accounts will be examined by the work team. The Party branch will go into secret session to examine its own performance up till now. The work team will take over the affairs of the village. It will root out commandism, hedonism, opportunism. It will re-examine the whole village's fanshen.

(HSUEH-CHEN *is staring at* HOU.)

Comrades, I am not saying you . . . you are thinking of the hours you have all worked, of the days, of the months, of the years, you have given. Don't. Don't think of yourself. Think of the people and how they are led.

(HSUEH-CHEN *and* CHENG-K'UAN *go out, saying nothing.*)

Wipe the slate clean and start again. Is that not right, Little Li?

LITTLE LI: Yes.

HOU: Ch'i-Yun?

CH'I-YUN: Yes.

HOU: The place is rotten. We must start again.

SECTION SEVEN

I

LITTLE LI *addresses the poorest in the village.* LAI-TZU, TING-FU, YUAN-LUNG, HUAN-CH'AO, OLD LADY WANG, HSIN-AI, T'AO-YUAN. HOU *sits beside* LITTLE LI *as he speaks.*

Slogan: **The Draft Agrarian Law**

LITTLE LI: Brothers and sisters, peasants of Long Bow.

In the course of the past two years this region has carried out a powerful and enthusiastic land reform programme. Over ten million people have already fanshened. But there are some areas where the peasants have only partially

fanshened or not fanshened at all. Now finally everyone
must fanshen.

In the past there were mistakes. There was favouritism.
People got more because they were soldiers, or because
they were cadres. Or because they were highly placed in
the movement.

Now the Draft Agrarian Law will correct all such mistakes
because it is firmly based on the slogan: 'Depend on the
poor peasant, unite with the middle peasant, destroy the
feudal system.'

Now what does this mean? It means the feudal system
will be finally eliminated and replaced with a new system
called 'Land to the Tiller'.

Lands and goods are to be redistributed on one basis and
one basis only: how much you have now and how many
there are in your family.

So no longer is it a question of what sort of person you
are, of whether you are thought to have helped or hindered
the movement. This time, those with merit will get some,
those without merit will get some. All landlords' property
will be divided and everyone will get a fair share. Now
how is this to be done?

It is to be done by a rigorous process of classification.
Each head of family in Long Bow will be classified
according to what he now has. If he is classified a poor
peasant, or hired labourer, he will be given something. If
he is classified a middle peasant, he will probably not be
touched. If he is classified a rich peasant or landlord, he
will have something taken away.

And this time it is you—the poor—the very poorest in the
village, who will be in charge of the classification process.
You will run the meetings. Each family head must come
before you and reveal his exact wealth and his exact needs.
You will discuss his report and decide his family's class
status.

But beware. You—the basic elements—are holding a knife
in your hands. We are at war. Class someone now as a
rich peasant and he becomes your enemy. Class someone

47

as a middle peasant and he becomes your ally. Class someone as a poor peasant and he becomes one of you. You must take care. For on these classifications will depend what everyone is to get, how they are to live for the rest of their lives.

(*The peasants applaud.*)

2

Slogan: **Self-report, Public Appraisal**

LAI-TZU: My name is Kuo Lai-tzu. I have two acres, there are four in my family. I have no children. I reap about ten bushels to the acre. And I don't have any kind of draft animals.

HOU: Discuss in groups.

(LAI-TZU *before the classification meeting. These are the poorest peasants again:* LAI-TZU, OLD LADY WANG, HUAN-CH'AO, T'AO-YUAN, TING-FU, YUAN-LUNG *and an old woman,* LI HSIN-AI. LI *and* HOU *are at the side, writing. The peasants are in distinct groups. The groups go into a huddle.*)

HOU: Report from your groups.

TING-FU: Poor peasant.

OLD LADY WANG: Poor peasant.

YUANG-LUNG: Poor peasant.

HOU: Poor peasant?

ALL: Yes, yes.

HSIN-AI: He hasn't even fanshened.

HOU: Poor peasant. I shall write it down. Next.

LAI-TZU: Told you.

(TING-FU *stands up.*)

TING-FU: Half an acre.

HOU: Name?

TING-FU: My name is Ting-fu. I have half an acre. No livestock, no implements. I have three sections of house.

YUAN-LUNG: Falling down.

TING-FU: And I share a privy, that's it.

OLD LADY WANG: Everyone knows him, he's a poor peasant.

LAI-TZU: He's the hardest worker in the village.

HOU: Poor peasant?

48

ALL: Yes, yes. Poor peasant.

HOU: Poor peasant. I shall write it down. Next.
(HUAN-CH'AO *steps up*.)

HUAN-CH'AO: My name is Chang Huan-ch'ao.

OLD LADY WANG: Yes well . . .

LITTLE LI: Let him speak.

HUAN-CH'AO: I'm a blacksmith. I have very little land because
I don't farm. I have four sections of house. I have a family
of four. That's all.

HOU: Discuss in groups.

OLD LADY WANG: There's no need. He's a middle peasant.

LITTLE LI: You must first discuss it in your group.

OLD LADY WANG: He's a middle peasant because he does so well
out of everyone . . .

YUAN-LUNG: How . . .

OLD LADY WANG: His prices are high and his work's rotten.
(*Laughter*.)

TUI-CHIN: He's certainly a terrible blacksmith.

HOU: Please.

HUAN-CH'AO: No, go on. Say what you like, I'm very interested.

OLD LADY WANG: You . . .

HUAN-CH'AO: Very happy to hear what you think.

OLD LADY WANG: We think . . .

HUAN-CH'AO: Yes?

OLD LADY WANG: We think you're a disgraceful blacksmith . . .

HUAN-CH'AO: I see, yes, that's very interesting.

OLD LADY WANG: And we wouldn't trust you to bang a nail up
an elephant's arsehole.

HUAN-CH'AO: I see. Yes. That's very clear.
(*Laughter*.)

HOU: Listen, it doesn't matter what sort of a blacksmith he is . . .

LAI-TZU: It matters to us.

OLD LADY WANG: You said a middle peasant is someone who
can make their own living . . .

HOU: That's not what I said. A middle peasant is someone who
himself rarely labours for others. He does. He hires his
labour to you. That makes him . . . (*He looks round for an
answer*.)

49

TING-FU: A worker.

LAI-TZU: What's a worker?

HOU: I don't think . . .

YUAN-LUNG: He's a poor peasant.

OLD LADY WANG: If we say he's a poor peasant, he'll get
something in the distribution and . . . I don't want him to
get anything.

LITTLE LI: That really isn't . . .

OLD LADY WANG: If he were a good blacksmith I'd be happy
for him to be a poor peasant.

HOU: Good and bad don't come into it.

YUANG-LUNG: Call him a poor peasant . . .

OLD LADY WANG: Who must improve his work.

HOU: You're a poor peasant who must improve your work.

LITTLE LI: Do we all agree?

TING-FU: No.

LITTLE LI: Why not?

TING-FU: He's a village worker.

LITTLE LI: We don't have that category.

TING-FU: Well you should. We can't call him a peasant,
peasants work on the land.

LITTLE LI: Well . . .

HOU: He's right.

TING-FU: You can't call him something he's not.

HOU: Thank you Ting-fu. We'll think about it. Huan-ch'ao, we
will defer your classification.

HUAN-CH'AO: Defer?

HOU: Yes. The next.

(HUAN-CH'AO *goes back to his seat.*)

HUAN-CH'AO: Just wait till it's your turn.

(T'AO-YUAN *steps up.*)

T'AO-YUAN: My name is Wang T'ao-yuan. Only two acres. No
wife, no animals. My land was given me in the first
distribution, two years ago. Before that I had no land at
all. I have one nephew to support. That's all.

HOU: Discuss in groups.

(*They do so.* T'AO-YUAN *smiles broadly while he waits.*)
Each group to report.

(*A representative stands up from each group.*)

LAI-TZU: Our group wants to ask about the past.

HOU: Yes.

LAI-TZU: You used to have a lot of money.

T'AO-YUAN: I have had money, yes.

LAI-TZU: I mean, I can remember when you didn't work.

T'AO-YUAN: Well . . .

LAI-TZU: How did you live?

T'AO-YUAN: This and that.

LAI-TZU: You sold heroin.

T'AO-YUAN: I smoked it myself.

LAI-TZU: You sold it . . .

T'AO-YUAN: In a way.

LAI-TZU: What way?

T'AO-YUAN: Just to make money. I only sold it to make money.

LAI-TZU: Well why else . . .

HOU: All right.

> (HOU *nods at the second group whose representative is* OLD
> LADY WANG.)

OLD LADY WANG: Tell us what happened to your wife.

T'AO-YUAN (*to* HOU): Is this . . .

HOU: Yes.

T'AO-YUAN: Well . . . I began smoking heroin in the famine
year and everything I had I spent on heroin. So when I
had nothing left I took my wife to Taiyuan. I was very
lucky, I managed to find a buyer quite quickly. He gave
me six bags of millet, so that sealed the deal.

OLD LADY WANG: And other people's wives, you sold them?

T'AO-YUAN: I helped sell them, occasionally.

OLD LADY WANG: And you got paid for this . . .

T'AO-YUAN: I was usually given heroin.

OLD LADY WANG: So your income came either from selling
heroin or selling other people's wives . . .

T'AO-YUAN: It's . . . one way of looking at it.

OLD LADY WANG: He should be classed as a landlord's running
dog. (*She sits.*)

HOU: Next group.

HUAN-CH'AO: We want to ask about the donkey. You had a

donkey?

T'AO-YUAN: Yes, I paid two hundred dollars for it.

HUAN-CH'AO: What happened to it?

T'AO-YUAN: It caught a cold, it died.

HUAN-CH'AO: I see. Thank you. (*He sits.*)

HOU: So.

OLD LADY WANG: May we ask what he now feels about selling his wife?

T'AO-YUAN: I feel . . . (*He begins to cry bitterly.*)

OLD LADY WANG: Really it was your own fault. You sold her and now you weep about it.

T'AO-YUAN: I'm not weeping for her. I'm weeping for my donkey.

(*Silence.*)

HOU: Classification. From your groups.

LAI-TZU: Middle peasant.

OLD LADY WANG: Rich peasant.

HUAN-CH'AO: Poor peasant.

(*Silence.*)

HOU: Discuss again.

3

(LITTLE LI *working at a desk with a candle on papers.* HOU *is staring out into the fields.*)

LITTLE LI: I have the results of the classification. Trying to make sense.

HOU: What is it?

LITTLE LI: One hundred and seventy-four families have been classed poor peasants.

HOU: Isn't that what we expected?

LITTLE LI: But only seventy-two have so far fanshened. It means there are one hundred families in the village who barely scrape a living. And I've nothing to give them. We found one rich peasant. One. It's not going to go very far. (*Pause.*) It's not land, there's enough land, one acre for every man, woman and child in Long Bow. It's resources. Animals, carts, implements, houses. That's what we need.

HOU: I've been over the village accounts to try and see if

anything was missed or stolen in the last distribution. Everyone says the cadres took too much, but I can't find anything.
(*Pause.*)

LITTLE LI: So what do we do next?

HOU: Expand the Poor Peasants' League.

LITTLE LI: It won't create *things*, comrade. (*Pause.*) I was at college, many years ago. People used to say China is poor, it's poor because it lacks fertilizer, it lacks machinery, it lacks insecticides, it lacks medical care. I used to say no, China is poor because it is unjust. (*Pause. Then he smiles.*)

HOU: We must prove it comrade.

LITTLE LI: Yes.

(*The house lights come up.*)

INTERVAL

53

ACT II

During the interval CHENG-K'UAN *and* HU HSUEH-CHEN *rehearse their speeches for the gate. You watch them prepare the words they will later deliver to the village.*

SECTION EIGHT

I

HOU *joins the cadres while* LITTLE LI *sets out the benches and tables.*

HOU: Are you ready?

CHENG-K'UAN: I'll never be ready. This is the most frightening day of my life.

HOU: Tell the truth and you have nothing to fear.

CHENG-K'UAN: I know that. But the people . . .

HOU: Trust them.

CHENG-K'UAN: I'd be happy to die tomorrow as long as I pass the gate.

(*From outside the hall we hear the delegates shout 'Purify the Party'. They are* YUAN-LUNG, LAI-TZU, HSIN-AI *and* HUAN-CH'AO *and* TING-FU. *They come in and are about to sit opposite the cadres when* HOU *begins to lead the singing of the internationale. The cadres all join in.* HOU *knows it best. Then they sit down.*)

HOU: The Communist Party is the servant of the people. To prove to you how seriously we take our charge, we have publicly posted the names of our members. It is no longer a secret organization. Now its members will appear before you, the delegates of the people, they will criticize their past actions and invite your grievances. They will then ask you to judge their future suitability for office.

Slogan: **The Gate**

CHENG-K'UAN: Comrades, on behalf of the Party I welcome you

54

the delegates of the people and hope that you will speak out clearly and fearlessly what you think. Certainly you need not fear any reprisal. In the past, you made me a cadre, but I am ready to admit that after fanshen I forgot my poor friends.

(YUAN-LUNG *gets up nervously to reply.*)

YUAN-LUNG: I am a poor peasant chosen as a delegate to help purify the Party. I hope every Party member will examine his past honestly. I cannot speak much. We are here because poor peasants do want to help the Party. So we can all fanshen thoroughly. (*He sits down, his ordeal over.*)

CHENG-K'UAN: So let me start. (*Pause.*) I was born in Long Bow but my family comes from Chih-chou. I grew up a Catholic, I was a hired labourer. I took part in struggle meetings as you know. Because of them I became Chairman of the Peasants' Association. This made me arrogant. For instance, when we had to collect tax grain we never talked it over with the people, we just met among ourselves and decided what each should give, then ordered people to hand over. I think this was wrong, it was obviously unfair. Also, I hit Tui-chin when he made a hurtful remark about my body, sheer bad temper and I have no excuse . . .

HSIN-AI: Tell us how much you won out of fanshen.

CHENG-K'UAN: Ah.

LAI-TZU: Yes.

CHENG-K'UAN: I won . . . more than the masses out of fanshen.

HSIN-AI: How much more?

CHENG-K'UAN: An acre of land. The best. Ten hundredweight of millet. And ten pieces of clothing. Good quality. (*Silence.*)

Then I joined the Party. I thought, I'm on the way up and nothing can stop me. I was working very hard and I thought what's the point of working hard if you don't get a little extra and live better than other people? It was wrong. It was wrong thinking. I've done so much that was wrong. I borrowed a pair of trousers from the public warehouse. They're worn out now. And I would like you

55

to help me. I would like to hear your grievances.

(*Pause.*)

LAI-TZU: When you took the village tax grain to Hukuan . . .

CHENG-K'UAN: Yes.

(*A known scandal.*)

LAI-TZU: Tell us about that.

CHENG-K'UAN: It was last year. There were two of us, I was with An-ho. We claimed three dollars personal expenses. But in fact I spent the money on cigarettes.

LAI-TZU: Why did you do that?

CHENG-K'UAN: Why?

LAI-TZU: Why did you buy cigarettes?

CHENG-K'UAN: Because my thinking was wrong. I thought I'm a cadre, I'm allowed to loll about and smoke cigarettes. I'm willing to return the money.

HUAN-CH'AO: How much?

CHENG-K'UAN: All of it.

HSIN-AI: Why?

CHENG-K'UAN: Why? Because . . .

HSIN-AI: You said two of you spent the money.

CHENG-K'UAN: Yes.

HSIN-AI: So why promise to pay it all back yourself? It just proves you're insincere.

CHENG-K'UAN: Four of us spent the money.

HSIN-AI: Then say so.

HUAN-CH'AO: Tell the truth.

HSIN-AI: You don't have to take the blame for what other people did.

CHENG-K'UAN: No.

HSIN-AI: And don't just agree with us.

CHENG-K'UAN: No.

HSIN-AI: Being criticized doesn't mean saying yes to everything.

CHENG-K'UAN: Yes. No.

HSIN-AI: Be objective and then criticize yourself.

CHENG-K'UAN: Yes.

(*Pause.*)

YUAN-LUNG: The candlesticks.

HSIN-AI: Yes, the silver candlesticks that were seized from the church . . .

CHENG-K'UAN: Yes.

HSIN-AI: What happened to them?

CHENG-K'UAN: They were sold.

HUAN-CH'AO: What happened to the money?

CHENG-K'UAN: It was distributed, to everyone. It was among the fruits.

HSIN-AI: It was a fortune, they were silver candlesticks.

CHENG-K'UAN: I don't think it was that much.

HSIN-AI: Tell the truth.

CHENG-K'UAN: I really can't remember.

HSIN-AI: What do you mean you don't remember—we can find out.

CHENG-K'UAN: Yes.

HSIN-AI: We can ask the landlord's wife, Wang Kuei-ching was business manager for the church. We can ask her.

HUAN-CH'AO: Well?

CHENG-K'UAN: Ask her.

Slogan: **They Talked For Six Hours**

HOU: Are you ready with the list?

CHENG-K'UAN: All the accusations you have made today. I hit four of you. I failed to consult you. I gave random orders. I took two dollars. Some clothing. I can offer no explanation for the money from the candlesticks. I thought of myself and not of serving the masses. Do you have any further grievances against me?

(*Pause.*)

HOU: Then you must decide how to deal with him. Cheng-k'uan, you must leave.

CHENG-K'UAN: I have loved my family. And my home. Now I love . . . the Communist Party. I shall wait patiently for the decision of the masses.

(*He goes out. A violent argument.*)

HSIN-AI: Suspend him from the Party.

TUI-CHIN: Yes.

HSIN-AI: Send him to the People's Court in Lucheng.

YUAN-LUNG: Huan-ch'ao?

HUAN-CH'AO: I think . . . just make him give everything back.

57

LAI-TZU: I agree, he's admitted his mistakes . . . that's what we wanted.

HSIN-AI: How can he give everything back when he says he doesn't remember?

HUAN-CH'AO: Just give it back.

HSIN-AI: We suffered, now he must suffer . . .

TUI-CHIN: Send him to the Court.

HSIN-AI: He must understand pain.

YUAN-LUNG: Why not just ask him to jump down the well?

HSIN-AI: Why not? I don't care if he starves to death.

TUI-CHIN: The Party was meant to serve the people . . .

HSIN-AI: So long as he gives back what he got during fanshen.

TUI-CHIN: It was meant to lead us to fanshen. But in fact only members of the Party really fanshened . . .

LAI-TZU: Then take something away.

TUI-CHIN: They became officials, just like feudal officials . . .

LAI-TZU: And now he's sorry.

TUI-CHIN: Cheng-k'uan climbed on our heads . . .

HSIN-AI: They all did.

TUI-CHIN: And now we must throw him out.

LAI-TZU: You're talking about one of the most popular men in the village . . .

TUI-CHIN: That just shows you.

LAI-TZU: You're talking about two dollars . . .

TUI-CHIN: I'm talking about why, why our leaders are rich, why we're still poor . . .

LAI-TZU: The Party . . .

TUI-CHIN: The Party has asked the people to decide, and this is what we decide. Send him to the Court.

HOU: The People's Court is for cases you cannot decide yourselves. Is that how you wish to be known? As the village that cannot decide the simplest case?

YUAN-LUNG: All we need to do is suspend him from office, just for a short time, and see if he really wants to reform.

TUI-CHIN: He should be thrown out of the Party.

YUAN-LUNG: No.

LAI-TZU: It was only two dollars . . .

TUI-CHIN: It's not what he did. It's what he let others do.

How did Yu-lai come to rule this town?

(*Pause.*)

HOU (*very quiet*): Yu-lai is in prison.

TUI-CHIN: Yes. Because you came with guns. And threw him in prison. Good. But up till then . . . where were our leaders? Well?

(*Pause.*)

HOU: So. Do we agree? You suspend him and then see if he corrects his behaviour. Is that what you want?

ALL: Yes.

HSIN-AI: He should never be a cadre again.

HUAN-CH'AO: Be quiet, you old shitbag.

HSIN-AI: He should be thrashed with a dogwhip.

HOU: Listen. Because you've been beaten you want to see him beaten. All right. Now we oppose beatings and this makes you bitter. You think unless we flay the skin off his back, he'll just carry on as before. But that's feudal behaviour. We are living in a new society. Are we not?

(*Pause.*)

YUAN-LUNG: Suspend him from office?

ALL: Yes.

(LITTLE LI *goes to get* CHENG-K'UAN.)

HOU: For how long?

YUAN-LUNG: Six months?

ALL: Yes.

(CHENG-K'UAN *returns.*)

YUAN-LUNG: We have decided that you have failed the gate, and that you must be suspended from office. However, in six months you will be given another chance to pass.

CHENG-K'UAN: I am happy to accept the decision of the masses.

(CHENG-K'UAN *returns to his seat.* HSUEH-CHEN *rises.*)

HSUEH-CHEN: I was a beggar, then a Party member.

YUAN-LUNG: Who are you?

(*He knows perfectly well.* HSUEH-CHEN *smiles.*)

HSUEH-CHEN: Hu Hsueh-chen, Secretary of the suspended Women's Association. I was a beggar, then a Party member, then in the Association. I have always struggled for equality for women . . .

YUAN-LUNG: Just tell us what you did wrong.

HSUEH-CHEN: Yes.

YUAN-LUNG: We all know what you did right . . .

HSUEH-CHEN: Yes.

YUAN-LUNG: You're always telling us.

HSUEH-CHEN: Yes.

YUAN-LUNG: Outstanding revolutionary cadre. Some cretin even painted you on the wall. So stick to what you did wrong.

HSUEH-CHEN: I think you'll find I've done as you ask. I have a list here. I can name the twenty-three occasions when I feel I may have impeded the revolution.

YUAN-LUNG: We'd like them in alphabetical order.

HSUEH-CHEN: I believe until you make a list, you don't really know yourself. And if you don't know yourself you can't criticize yourself. And if you can't criticize yourself both privately and in front of the masses, you can't be a Communist.

(*Quiet. The peasants all look at her, taking account.*)

There is the occasion I shouted at Fa-liang. There is the occasion I called Chuan-e a whore and burnt her best dress because I thought it . . . unsuitable for a woman. There is the occasion I hit Tao-yuan for giving a girl heroin. There is the occasion I tried to get a meeting postponed so I could canvass . . .

HUAN-CH'AO: This is pointless.

HSUEH-CHEN: There is the occasion . . .

HUAN-CH'AO: It's pointless reading it out. We know it'll all be there, it'll all be listed, anything we can think of, but it won't . . .

HOU: What?

HUAN-CH'AO: It won't—it won't—it's not what she did, it's that —look on her face . . .

HSUEH-CHEN: Please . . .

HUAN-CH'AO: Of course she's got her list, it's perfect, but her face . . .

LAI-TZU: You can't blame a woman . . .

HUAN-CH'AO: Look at it, just look at it. She knows she's going to pass, that's what I can't bear, and it shows in her face.

HSUEH-CHEN: I promise you, I don't know.

HUAN-CH'AO: Look at you. All the time. I have suffered more than you. I know more than you. I'm a better person than you.

HSUEH-CHEN: I don't think that.

HUAN-CH'AO: Round the lips, just a slight turn at the side, and your head . . .

HOU: We can't pass or fail people's faces . . .

HUAN-CH'AO: Of course we can. That's just what we should do. Why does everyone bristle the moment she comes in? Because of that look that says she's a leader. That's why the people resent her.

HOU: Sit down.

(HUAN-CH'AO *sits.*
Pause.)

HOU: Hsueh-chen?

HSUEH-CHEN: I submit to the people. I will try to correct my face.

2

Slogan: **The Results Of The Gate**

(COMRADE HOU *before the people of Long Bow.*)

HOU: We have heard every accusation you have to make against your leaders. Twenty-six members of the Party have appeared before you. Twenty-two have passed the gate, four have failed. Four more still in jail after the attack on a member of the work team have not yet appeared. We have found fifty-five cases of beating. A hundred and three cases of personal selfishness and corrupt practice.

Seventeen cases of illicit sexual relations of which half may be called rape. Eleven cases of forgetting one's class. We also found in spite of rumour that the cadres of Long Bow got very little more in fanshen than the people.

Tomorrow the work team goes to a regional conference in Lucheng. I shall be able to tell the secretary how we have purged the Party of wrongdoing, and how you have begun the process of purification. I shall be able to say with

61

pride: in Long Bow the Party submits to the People.

SECTION NINE

1

At once the tolling of an enormous temple bell. Underneath it sitting on a bench the work team in a row. Sober.

Slogan: **The Trip To Lucheng County**

(AN OFFICIAL *appears to usher them in.*)

OFFICIAL: Secretary Ch'en will speak to the Long Bow delegation before the conference begins. He hasn't got very long.

(THE OFFICIAL *leads them through to where* CH'EN *is at his desk. The team are left standing.* CH'EN *shakes hands with* HOU.)

CH'EN: Comrade Hou. Good. Have you prepared your report?

HOU: Yes.

CH'EN: Good. It will be called . . . as soon as possible. For the moment, the matter of Yu-lai and his friends . . .

HOU: Yes.

CH'EN: Why was he arrested?

HOU: There was an attack . . .

CH'EN: I know.

HOU: On a member of the work team.

CH'EN: The arrest was a mistake.

(*Silence.*)

HOU: There was evidence . . .

CH'EN: I have heard rumours that the four cadres have been tried at a mass meeting and shot.

HOU: That's not true.

CH'EN: Of course not. The point is I have heard it, peasants throughout Lucheng County have heard it . . .

HOU: I can't . . .

CH'EN: Let me finish my point. Thirty miles away from Long Bow the rumours are credited. And they lend currency to the belief that the cadres were guilty. And that undermines the work of every cadre in the County. There was not enough evidence for an arrest.

HOU: There was a towel.

CH'EN: Saying 'good morning'. I know. My own towel says 'good morning'. I doubt if there is a village in all China that does not have twenty towels saying 'good morning'. (*Pause.*) You arrested them on the basis of rumour and suspicion. You had no firm evidence. The County police have already decided to release them. (*Pause.*) It seems you made your minds up about the village before you even got there. And then you accepted the worst version of everything you heard. Isn't it true you suspended all the cadres the very first day you were there? Isn't it true you put the whole Party branch under supervision and took control of the village yourselves? Isn't it true that by the second day you were publicly examining the village accounts before you commanded any support among the people? And from what I've heard of the Long Bow gate you countenanced every slur the people could bring against their leaders. Cheng-k'uan failed the gate because he was suspected of misusing money from the sale of candlesticks.

HOU: Yes.

CH'EN: We've looked into that. The candlesticks weren't even silver. They were pewter. They were worth very little. And yet you went to Wang's widow for evidence, you went to a class enemy for testimony against a cadre. We have a name for what you did. We call it Left extremism. (CH'EN *picks up a document from his desk.*) Here is a report prepared by the third administrative district of the Taihang subregion. Your mistakes are already listed in that. You have sought support only from the poor peasants, thereby neglecting the middle peasants. You've treated Party members as if they were class enemies. Everything the poor peasants wanted you have believed and tried to give them. You have elevated their point of view to the status of a line. That line is in clear opposition to the official policy of the Party.

(*Silence.*)

I shall be using the work of your team as an example to

the whole conference of Left deviation. I hope after criticism we shall be able to correct your faults.
(*Silence.*)
Shall we go in.

2

(*Among the ruins of a bell tower. Sitting by a ruined wall is* CH'I-YUN *cooking soup.* LITTLE LI *appears quietly.*)

CH'I-YUN: Is he still talking?

LITTLE LI: Secretary Ch'en? Yes. He's been talking four hours.

CH'I-YUN: What are we to do?

LITTLE LI: Work teams throughout the County are to return to their villages. The Secretary feels too many middle peasants have been pushed over to the enemy side. We need all the allies we can get. So he is introducing a new standard in classification. The line between the middle and the rich peasant is to be redefined. We must fix it precisely. It's harder. More complex.
(CHANG CH'UER *comes in, rubbing his hands.*)

CHANG CH'UER: Is there something to eat?

CH'I-YUN: Not yet.

CHANG CH'UER: I'm hungry. What were you talking about?

LITTLE LI: The new classification.

CHANG CH'UER: Ah yes. Classification.
(*Silence.*)
Why do you never talk about yourself, Little Li?

LITTLE LI: Mmmh.

CHANG CH'UER: We think about ourselves. All the time, we all do . . .

LITTLE LI: I . . .

CHANG CH'UER: I don't know why we always talk about the poor, the poor peasants. Here we are looking miserable as goats, and it's not because we're worried about the poor, it's because Secretary Ch'en has shat all over us.

CH'I-YUN (*smiles*): Yes.

CHANG CH'UER: Come on cabbage. (*Pause.*) I really wouldn't mind being poor. It's a good life when you compare it with being a cadre.

64

(HOU *has appeared, confident.*)

HOU: You all heard the Secretary. I have details of the new system here. I don't think it should give us too much trouble. We shall go back to Long Bow tomorrow. What's for supper?

CHANG CH'UER: We can't go back.

(*Pause.*)

LITTLE LI: We must talk.

HOU: I think I should decide when we're to talk . . .

LITTLE LI: It's a warm night. Look at the stars. I suggest the form is self-criticism, yes?

HOU: I don't think . . .

CHANG CH'UER: Only if it's honest.

LITTLE LI: Of course.

CHANG CH'UER: From everybody.

HOU: What do you mean?

CHANG CH'UER: We can't go back till we've spoken.

(*Pause.* HOU *wanders away, serious now, to think what this means.* CH'I-YUN *speaks very quietly, regretful.*)

CH'I-YUN: You've lost the trust of your team. Sit down.

(*Pause.* HOU *sits.*)

HOU: Supper?

LITTLE LI: After. Criticism first. Ch'i-Yun?

CH'I-YUN: I think most of what Ch'en said is true. When I went to Long Bow I did think poverty was everything. I just looked for rags and fleabites, I thought the smellier the better; lice-ridden, shit-stained old men I thought wonderful, I can't get enough of it, I'm really doing the job. And I believed everything they said, every accusation made against the Party. That was wrong. I lacked objectivity. (*She looks round, handing it on like a baton.*)

LITTLE LI: From the very start we persecuted the . . .

CHANG CH'UER: Criticize yourself.

LITTLE LI: From the very start I persecuted the village cadres. I was over-harsh, I assumed everything was true. I kept telling the village they were poor because the cadres had taken all the fruits. But really, how much did they take? And if it were all divided up, what difference would it make to the whole distribution? (LITTLE LI *looks at* CHANG CH'UER.)

CHANG CH'UER: For a long time I've been thinking mostly about myself. After I was attacked I was very ill, the medicine the doctor gave me was very expensive. So I asked my neighbours for help, but they just said, you're a cadre and cadres should serve the people like oxen. Now I'm away from home, from my wife, from my children, and no one is helping me in the mutual aid scheme while I'm away because they refuse to help cadres. All the time, all the time I'm thinking my land is rotting and the people do not trust their leaders . . . I'm a servant of the people but sometimes . . . I find the people very hard to like.

(CHANG CH'UER *looks up, the baton passed.* HOU *silent.*)

LITTLE LI: Comrade . . .

HOU: I'm not a good leader, I know that. I do try.

CHANG CH'UER: Honest, we said, honest.

HOU: I know I'm not clever . . .

CHANG CH'UER: We said honest. Not humble. Humble isn't honest. Humble's humble. Humble's a way of not being criticized . . .

HOU: I do try . . .

CHANG CH'UER: Whenever we've tried to criticize you, you just say I know it's terrible, I'm just such a terrible person, you say yes, yes I'm sorry of course I know I'm so weak . . . but that doesn't solve anything.

HOU: I lie awake at night . . .

CH'I-YUN: That's just what's wrong, don't you see? It's useless lying awake at night. It's no help to anyone, it's subjective. Your work style is undemocratic.

HOU: I thought this was to be self-criticism.

CHANG CH'UER: We can't go back if you won't talk to us.

HOU: I took the job on very proud, very confident, then I began to realize it was more difficult than anything I had done in my life. I lost my nerve.

CHANG CH'UER: Why didn't you . . .

LITTLE LI (*stops him*): Ah.

HOU: I became afraid to consult you. I felt Little Li was just waiting for me to put a foot wrong. I thought I must be strong or they'll think ill of me. That's what leaders always think. That's what leaders are. Do this. Do that. And at the back of the head . . . what do they think of me? (*He smiles.*) After Ch'en . . . after what Ch'en said to us today I realized I'm not suited to the job, I've led the team badly and I must resign.

CH'I-YUN: Oh no.

LITTLE LI: No.

CHANG CH'UER: Wrong, wrong, wrong.

LITTLE LI: Do you understand nothing?

CH'I-YUN: What rubbish.

LITTLE LI: 'I resign.'

HOU: I feel . . .

CHANG CH'UER: Always the hero, you . . . always want to be the hero. 'I resign.'

LITTLE LI: 'I resign.'

CHANG CH'UER: Wonderful.

HOU: I'm sure . . .

LITTLE LI: I? I? Who is this I? The I who said I don't want my decisions questioned?

(*Silence.*)

HOU: Yes. That I.

(*Silence.*)

CH'I-YUN: We have to go back tomorrow and set about reclassifying the village. It will not . . . go down well. No one will light fires for our return. We will have to explain, discuss, report, evaluate, classify, post results, then listen to appeals, explain again, discuss again, classify again, post revised results. How can we do it if we are thinking of ourselves?

(*Silence.*)

Right now we are thinking life is easier at home. But that is because we have been badly led.

HOU: I . . .

CH'I-YUN: Yes.

(*Silence.*)

Why do we live in this world? Is it just to eat and sleep

67

and lead a worthless life? That is the landlord and rich peasant point of view. Enjoy life, waste food and clothes, have children. But a Communist works not only for his own life: he has offered everything to the service of his class. If he finds one poor brother suffering from hunger and cold, he has not done his duty. Comrade.
(*Silence.*)
You should talk to us more.

CHANG CH'UER: It doesn't solve my problem.

CH'I-YUN: Nothing will solve your problem.

CHANG CH'UER: Thank you.

CH'I-YUN: Except working harder.

CHANG CH'UER: I work eighteen hours a day.

CH'I-YUN: Work twenty. You can if you want to. If we make you want to. But Comrade Hou must give us a lead.

HOU: Yes.
(*Silence. He is at the end of his personality.*)

HOU: What should I do?

CH'I-YUN: You have just given us a totally inadequate account of your work as team leader. You must make specific accusations against yourself. Only then will we begin to get at the truth. Only then will we begin to work as a team. You must go back over every event. You must tell us how and where and when you went wrong. When you began not to trust us. You must trace back over everything, every detail, every bad thought.

HOU: Yes.
(*Silence.*)
I have led the team badly.

CH'I-YUN: Be specific.

HOU: Once . . .

SECTION TEN

I

Three different households.

TUI-CHIN *is sitting outside his house.* CHENG-K'UAN *is staring into a bucket containing a dead child. And in* WEN-TE's *house* HSIEN-E *is*

68

working. Meanwhile the work team try to go about their business.
Slogan: **Yu-lai and Wen-te Return To Long Bow**

(YU-LAI *and* WEN-TE *walk down the village street,* TUI-CHIN
*withdraws indoors and prepares to go to bed. As they look
around . . .*)

YU-LAI: What is it?

WEN-TE: It's called chewing-gum. Someone gave me it in
prison.

YU-LAI: Ah.

(WEN-TE *gives him the bit he has been chewing.* YU-LAI *puts
it in.* CHANG CH'UER *goes to* TUI-CHIN's *house.* YU-LAI *smiles
at* WEN-TE.)

YU-LAI: What a place. Why did we return?

CHANG CH'UER: Comrade. There is a meeting tonight.
Classification.

TUI-CHIN: I've been classified.

CHANG CH'UER: To help classify others.

TUI-CHIN: I have my own classification, that's enough. I'm
tired and I'm going to bed.

CHANG CH'UER: Tui-chin.

TUI-CHIN: Don't raise your voice, I'll report you.

(YU-LAI *sits down outside the house and starts to polish his
Luger.*)

YU-LAI: Go and find your wife.

(WEN-TE *goes into the house.*)

CHANG CH'UER: We need to form a new Peasants' League.

TUI-CHIN: We've got a Poor Peasants' League.

CHANG CH'UER: An official league this time, not a provisional.

TUI-CHIN: Ah.

CHANG CH'UER: To carry out a new classification, so we can
form a Provisional Peasants' Association.

TUI-CHIN: We've got a Peasants' Association.

CHANG CH'UER: A new Peasants' Association . . .

TUI-CHIN: What for?

CHANG CH'UER: A new gate.

(*Pause.*)

TUI-CHIN: I'm tired.

(TUI-CHIN *turns away.* WEN-TE *faces* HSIEN-E *inside the*

house. YU-LAI *still sits outside.*)

HSIEN-E: Wen-te.

YU-LAI: Tell her we're hungry.

WEN-TE: My father says we're hungry.

HSIEN-E: There's corn.

WEN-TE: She says there's corn.

YU-LAI: Rabbit. In a stew. With garlic. And leeks. Pork.
Shrimp. Onions. Tell her. Dumplings with herbs.
Beancurd. Tell her. Tell her to ask her friends in the
village, tell her to visit their homes, suggest . . . they give
us . . . their food.

(HSIEN-E *stares at* WEN-TE.)

HSIEN-E: There's some corn.

(WEN-TE *smashes* HSIEN-E *hard across the face. Then beats
her.*)

TUI-CHIN: It's not as if anyone else'll be there . . .

CHANG CH'UER: That's not true.

TUI-CHIN: Nobody obeys orders here any more, what's the
point?

CHANG CH'UER: Tui-chin.

TUI-CHIN: I was among the keenest, comrade. Among the first.
Then when you came, you told us to denounce corrupt
leaders. And I did. I denounced Yu-lai while he was in
prison. And now he's been released. Do you think he
doesn't know? Do you think he isn't waiting for revenge?
Feel my back. I'm sweating.

CHANG CH'UER: We had no choice.

TUI-CHIN: At least before they would have killed him.

(*He prepares for bed.* CH'I-YUN *crosses to* CHENG-K'UAN's
house. YU-LAI *calls to* WEN-TE *inside the house.*)

YU-LAI: What does she say?

WEN-TE: She says yes, certainly, at once, of course, she's just
going, sorry to be so long, are you sure that's all you want?
(WEN-TE *thrashes wildly at* HSIEN-E *with his belt. She runs
out of the house, at great speed and away.*)

CH'I-YUN: Cheng-k'uan. Why is there no one at the meeting?
Cheng-k'uan.

CHANG CH'UER: We will organize another gate. To bring Yu-lai

70

and Wen-te before the people. Confront them with their crimes. Sort everything out. Will you testify? Will you denounce them before the gate?

TUI-CHIN: Yu-lai and Wen-te are innocent. Of everything. That's what I'll say.

(WEN-TE *comes out of the house. Stands beside his father.*)

WEN-TE: She's gone to get the food.

TUI-CHIN: I trusted you. We all did.

(YU-LAI *throws the chewing-gum to the ground.*)

YU-LAI: This stuff doesn't taste.

CH'I-YUN: I know it's hard. And it's tiring, Cheng-k'uan. But you must never give up.

CHENG-K'UAN: I buried the cord. I was told to bury the cord.

CHANG CH'UER: Are you coming to the meeting?

(*Silence.* CH'I-YUN *uncovers the child.*)

CHANG CH'UER: I promise, I promise to try and help.

CH'I-YUN: Tell me what happened.

CHENG-K'UAN: Our child was born in a wash-basin six days ago. None of us knew it was coming so it just fell into a dirty basin at my wife's feet. We had nothing to cut the cord. She was bent forward, the child was filthy, my wife couldn't move. At first I couldn't find the midwife. Then after an hour she came, with an old pair of scissors.

(*Pause.* CHANG CH'UER *leaves* TUI-CHIN's *house.* TUI-CHIN *goes to bed.*)

CHENG-K'UAN: How can we go on? I'm tired. Everyone says I've fanshened, but what's changed? Where are the doctors? How I long for money. Doctors. Scalpels. Clothes, clean clothes.

CH'I-YUN: They'll come.

(CH'I-YUN *turns away.* YU-LAI *looks up smiling at* CHANG CH'UER.)

YU-LAI: What's the matter? Can't get anyone to your meetings?

CHANG CH'UER: They're frightened.

(*Holding the gun with both hands at arms' length,* YU-LAI *walks towards* CHANG CH'UER.)

YU-LAI: Use force.

CHANG CH'UER: They're frightened of you.

(YU-LAI *steps back. He is genuinely angry.* CH'I-YUN *has joined them outside.* YU-LAI *yells at the top of his lungs, red, demented.*)

YU-LAI: Has anyone. In the village. Any charge. Against me. Will anyone. Speak.

(*A silence. Then* YU-LAI *laughs and fires his gun in the air.* CH'I-YUN *turns away.* YU-LAI *looks up smiling at* CHANG CH'UER.)

YU-LAI: Good night.

WEN-TE: Good night.

(*They go into the house.*)

CH'I-YUN: Until finally after many months a young bride led the way.

2

(HSIEN-E *crosses the village at night.*)

HSIEN-E: I'll give evidence at the gate.

CH'I-YUN: Hsien-e.

HSIEN-E: Against my father-in-law Yu-lai. And against my husband Wen-te.

CH'I-YUN: Let me light this lamp.

HSIEN-E: No. If I testify . . .

CH'I-YUN: Yes.

HSIEN-E: I must never see him again. They'd kill me.

CH'I-YUN: Yes.

HSIEN-E: And I shall want a divorce.

(*Pause.*)

CH'I-YUN: You must go to the County . . .

HSIEN-E: I know. But first I must have the backing of the Women's Association, you must promise me that . . .

CH'I-YUN: No one has ever been divorced in Long Bow, the men will be against it . . .

HSIEN-E: Of course.

CH'I-YUN: And the older women.

HSIEN-E: Wen-te beat me. And Yu-lai. With a mule-whip. Often to within an inch of my life. I must have the backing of the Association. If I am not given a divorce, I will kill myself. (*Pause.*) What do you say?

72

CH'I-YUN: I say, come in, sleep here, never go home again. We will look after you. Plead your case to the Women's Association, then appear at the gate. I say that women . . . are half of China.
(*The banner unfurls to read* **Women Are Half Of China**. *An embrace. The scene breaks.*)

3

HOU: To bring before the gate those who have so far avoided it.

Slogan: **The Second Gate**

(*This gate is in the church. Present are* WEN-TE, HSIEN-E *and* YU-LAI. *At the side are* COMRADE HOU *and* LITTLE LI. *Delegates to the gate are* TUI-CHIN, CHENG-K'UAN, HSIN-AI *and* HUAN-CH'AO.)

HOU: Wang Wen-te, son to Wang Yu-lai, suspended Head of Police. You must criticize yourself.

WEN-TE: I don't want to . . . everything. I'll just list the things. I once beat Hsi-le because he was moaning about fanshen, saying it had been a mistake, so I rapped him about the face a couple of times. That was wrong, I should have talked to him. Also, bitterness. I admit to cursing the work team, when they sent me wrongfully to prison. In public I called them cunts. I said . . . Comrade Hou was a cunt. That was wrong. Also . . .

(YU-LAI *comes into the meeting late. Walks down the aisle. Sits down. Everyone watches him.*)

WEN-TE: I once . . . gave Huan-ch'ao a thrashing because of some silly gossip.

HUAN-CH'AO: It wasn't gossip, it was true.

HOU: Let him speak.

WEN-TE: I know that was wrong.

HUAN-CH'AO: Why did you beat me?

HOU: Let him finish.

WEN-TE: I think that's all. I don't think anybody here would have . . . any serious things to add. I would be surprised.

(*He looks at them all daring them to speak.* HUAN CH'AO *rises and goes right up to him.*)

HUAN-CH'AO: Turtle's egg. Donkey's tool. Your mother's

73

stinking cunt. (*He puts a finger in his face and shouts.*) You beat me because I told the truth. I said you beat your wife. That's why you left me for dead. Because I told the truth.

(*He tries to strangle him.* HOU *separates them.*)

HOU: Get him off. Get him off.

HUAN-CH'AO (*screaming*): I was left for dead. (*He is dragged off. Then looks round.*) Why? Why have you stopped me? Am I the only one? Am I the only man in Long Bow? I risk my life to accuse them. And you . . . when you find my body in a ditch, you will know everything.

(*He sits down.* YU-LAI *speaks very quietly.*)

YU-LAI: The man is mad. There's no case to answer.

(HSIEN-E *stands at once. Her assurance and command are stunning.*)

WEN-TE: Not her.

HSIEN-E: When I was ten, my parents were starving, they sold me to be engaged to Wen-te. In return they got grain and money. I had to go and live in Yu-lai's home. He starved me, I had to go into the fields to find herbs to stay alive. They gave me only water. When I was fourteen, they made me marry him. After the marriage they often locked me in the house for weeks. Wen-te locked the doors and whipped me with a mule-whip. His father was free with me. I have made up my mind to divorce him, I have the backing of the Women's Association. Have I said enough?

HOU: Did you beat her?

(WEN-TE *looks at* YU-LAI. YU-LAI *almost nods.*)

WEN-TE: Once or twice.

HOU: Why?

YU-LAI: Because she used to flirt in the cornfield, with other men. She was late with supper because she'd been whoring . . .

(TUI-CHIN *like a barrack-room lawyer.*)

TUI-CHIN: How old was your wife when you married her?

WEN-TE: She . . .

HSIEN-E: Fourteen.

WEN-TE: Fifteen.

YU-LAI: Sixteen.

WEN-TE: Sixteen.

TUI-CHIN: How did you get a licence at the district office?

HSIEN-E: He ordered me to say I was sixteen.

TUI-CHIN: Is that true? (*Pause.*) Is that true? (*He turns to* HSIEN-E.) Why did you agree to lie?

WEN-TE: Because she wanted to marry me of course.

TUI-CHIN: Then you admit she lied. (*Pause.*) Why did you agree?

HSIEN-E: Because they threatened my parents.

TUI-CHIN: How?

HSIEN-E: They threatened to denounce them as Kuomintang agents.

HUAN-CH'AO: Anyone who disobeyed them was called a spy.

HSIN-AI: Yes, that's how they dealt with everyone.

HOU: What do you say?

WEN-TE: It's . . . very hard to remember. I can't remember. I can't remember the answers. (*Pause.*) Criticize me. While I try to remember the answers.

Slogan: **They Talked For Eight Hours**

(*Change of pitch.* WEN-TE *is broken, muttering inaudibly.* YU-LAI *is frozen, a Buddha. The pace is furious.*)

TUI-CHIN: The opinions of the masses pile up like a mountain.

CHENG-K'UAN: The list of charges is now five foot long.

WEN-TE: I can't remember anything.

TUI-CHIN: He doesn't understand, he doesn't even know what's going on. (*He is delighted.*)

WEN-TE: Criticize me. Please.

HSIN-AI: Kick him out of the Party and send him to the County Court.

ALL: Yes.

HOU: Do you agree to that, Wen-te?

WEN-TE: Of course. Yes. Send me to the Court. I deserve it. I have betrayed the masses.

HSIEN-E: And will you grant me a divorce?

(*He looks up at her. Then bursts into a fit, banging his head on the ground on each 'Never'.*)

WEN-TE: Never. I will never agree to that until the last minute

75

of my life. Never. Never. Never.

HSIEN-E: You must.

WEN-TE: I will never beat you again.

HSIEN-E: He's lying.

WEN-TE: Never.

HSIEN-E: What if you beat me to death?

WEN-TE: I take an oath before the people.

HOU (*quiet*): That's enough, Hsien-e. He won't give you a divorce.

HSIEN-E: But . . .

HOU: We can't help.

(*Silence. She sits down.*)

The case demands . . . the severest punishment. Party members have a trust which you have betrayed. The people say you must go to the County Court.

(YU-LAI *gets up, his patience exhausted.*)

YU-LAI: Bonehead. Plank. Donkey's anus. I coached you for three days and you didn't get one answer right.

(WEN-TE *begins to cry.*)

HOU: Next before the gate. Wang Yu-lai.

(*The people look glad.*

Three tableaux of accusation. Then he is thrown down in the cadres' office by LITTLE LI. *The rest scatter.*)

4

LITTLE LI: You'll sleep in here. We'll keep you here until your trial.

YU-LAI: I want to die. I want to be left to die. There's nothing. Going back to prison, there's nothing.

LITTLE LI: You have betrayed the people. And you have failed the gate. There should be nothing.

YU-LAI: What can I do?

LITTLE LI: You should have told the truth, then you would have had some chance.

YU-LAI: If I'd told the truth they would have killed me.

(*Enter* CHANG CH'UER *and* CH'I-YUN, *very up.*)

CH'I-YUN: Where is he?

CHANG CH'UER: The people are cheering. The people have just

cheered us through the streets.

CH'I-YUN: There's a celebration tonight.

CHANG CH'UER: The work we can do.

(COMRADE HOU *comes in with* SECRETARY LIU.)

HOU: Secretary Liu, this is the man. Members of the work team this is Secretary Liu. He has come from Taihang to check on the progress of the work.

LITTLE LI: Comrade.

CH'I-YUN: Comrade.

LIU: Why is he crying? (*Pause.*) Tell me why you are crying.

YU-LAI: I want to die.

LIU: Why?

YU-LAI: There's nothing.

LIU: Nothing?

YU-LAI: Nothing for me.

LIU: Why?

YU-LAI: If I'm sent to the People's Court, I'll be shot.

LIU: Who told you that?

YU-LAI: If I confess everything, I'll be lynched. Or they'll throw me out of the Party and that's as bad as being shot.

LIU: Yes.

YU-LAI: People hate me, they want me dead.

LIU: You can still decide your fate. It's up to you. I know people who have done much worse than you. They have faced the people honestly and the people have accepted them again as leaders.

YU-LAI: I can't face living in this . . .

LIU: You can. Everyone can face everything.

YU-LAI: The people hate me.

LIU: No. They hate what you've done. (*Pause.*) The people have voted to send you to the Court. You are not yet in prison. Walk down the street. Try it.

(YU-LAI *goes.*)

How did this happen? You let him lose hope. How could you? Never, never let a man lose hope. It's a waste, to the Party. To the people. It's easy, it's so easy to stamp something out. It's what they do in every country in the world. They cure diseases by killing the patient. But we

. . . are going to save the patient.

CHANG CH'UER: You're going to let him loose?

LIU: Why not?

LITTLE LI: He and his son terrorized the village . . .

LIU: Ah I see so you thought get them out of the way and everything will be all right . . .

LITTLE LI: The people . . .

LIU: But it won't comrade. You can't smooth trouble over, it will come back at you, always it will appear somewhere else unless you dig out the root.

CH'I-YUN: The people wanted rid of him.

LIU: Of course . . .

LITTLE LI: And we proved, we proved today we could remove their fears . . .

LIU: Of course you did, that's the easy part . . .

LITTLE LI: We proved today the Party is ready to purify its own ranks . . .

LIU: No. You proved the Party could be brutal and wasteful. There is a school in Changchih for cadres who cannot pass the gate. A place where they can be re-educated, taken out of their own lives, given a chance to think, to learn, to be objective. He should go there. He should not go to prison. On no account should he be thrown out of the Party. (*Pause.*) It's a practical question, you must say what you think.

CHANG CH'UER: Send him to the school. We can use him.

HOU: Yes. Our thinking was wrong.

CH'I-YUN: Yes.

LITTLE LI: No. We said purify the Party, we promised that. Now we mustn't go back. The people need to see him punished.

LIU: Or is it you who needs that?

LITTLE LI: We worked so hard to organize that meeting.

LIU: And you want a reward?

LITTLE LI: I want justice.

LIU: Well?

HOU: The overall feeling of the team is strongly for reforming the man.

78

LIU: Good.

LITTLE LI: If men like Yu-lai can remain as Communists then what is the point of the campaign?

LIU: There are no breakthroughs in our work. There is no 'just do this one thing and we will be there'. There is only the patient, daily work of re-making people. Over each hill, another hill. Over that hill, a mountain. The Party needs Yu-lai because he is clever and strong, and reformed will be of more value to the people than if he had never been corrupted. We must save him. We can use him. He can be reformed.

SECTION ELEVEN

I

SECRETARY CH'EN *addresses the delegates from the platform.*

Slogan: **The Second Lucheng Conference**

CH'EN: Comrades. The twenty-year war is almost over. Chiang Kai-shek's armies are doomed. A People's Republic is within our reach. And so we have come to a turning point. And we have called you in today because many wrong ideas have been shared and many wrong actions have been taken.

At our last meeting in Lucheng you were told that land reform was far from complete. We have now discovered, after surveys of the area, that this was wrong, that the feudal system in our County has been fundamentally abolished. The peasants have in the main fanshened. The surveys show that in Lucheng County the poor peasants now farm an average of four-fifths of an acre each, the middle peasants slightly less, the rich peasants one-sixth of an acre each. So there is only one land problem remaining and it is the very opposite of what you imagine: the attack has been overdone.

Think back all of you to the Draft Agrarian Law. Think back to Article 16. 'In places where the land has already been distributed before the announcement of the law, the land need not be further redistributed.'

79

Is this not such a place? Had we not already spontaneously and in advance of the Party undertaken land reform at the end of the Japanese occupation, BEFORE the law was announced?

Work teams have been applying land reform policy long after land reform has occurred. Because some people still have less, work teams have continued to hunt for non-existent wealth. They have continued to blame and persecute old rank-and-file cadres. And they have frightened and alienated many middle peasants, men who were never exploiters but who have always been our allies, and should have been treated as such.

Now how did this wrong line come about? It came about through an excess of zeal. It came about through blind utopianism, because so many work teams were ensnared by the idea of equality, of wanting to give everybody in China equal shares. This idea is dangerous. It encourages wrong standards. It has been condemned by Marx, by Engels, by Lenin, by Stalin. It is Leftism.

Equality cannot be established by decree. Even if we could give everyone an equal share, how long would it last? The strong, the ruthless would soon climb to the top; the weak and the sick would sink to the bottom. Only in the future when all land and productive wealth is finally held in common and we produce in great abundance will equality be possible.

So we have been judging fanshen by the wrong principles. We have taken absolute equality as our banner. We have tried to be charitable. We have tried to give everyone everything they need. We have tried to be god.

Land reform can have only one standard and it is not equality. It is the abolition of the feudal system. And that we have achieved.

Now we know from history that whenever victory draws near it's easy for cadres to become adventurist, to alienate their allies, to persecute creators of wealth, to make impossible leftist demands. This is counter-revolutionary, because it pits working people against working people and endangers the success of the whole movement.

We must rein ourselves in. Above all in Lucheng County we must begin the work of returning goods and land to those middle peasants from whom we have taken too much. And we must ensure that landlords are given enough land to make a living.

(LITTLE LI *gets up and leaves*.)

How this is to be done we shall discuss in the coming days.

2

(LITTLE LI *pacing up and down in the square is joined by the rest of the work team*.)

LITTLE LI: It's insane. It's totally insane.

HOU: Li . . .

LITTLE LI: The policy has changed again.

Slogan: **They Talked For Sixteen Hours**

LITTLE LI: We are to go back to the village, we are to tell the people Article 16 has been overlooked, this means the fanshen was finished two years ago, you've had all you're going to get, in fact you're going to have to give some back.

CH'I-YUN: You're frightened of the people, Little Li. Frightened to admit you made a mistake.

LITTLE LI: I didn't make it. He did.

CH'I-YUN: Who?

LITTLE LI: Ch'en.

HOU: Then tell him.

LITTLE LI: They just change the policy whenever it suits them.

HOU: I shall go and find Secretary Ch'en and tell him the Long Bow delegation wishes to speak to him.

LITTLE LI: Don't be ridiculous. He won't even come.

HOU: I shall tell him you have a criticism. I've no doubt he'll come. (*He goes out*.)

LITTLE LI: If the Party can make mistakes like that, what is there for us to cling to?

CHANG CH'UER: I don't feel that. I feel as if a great rock has been lifted from my back. These last few months I'd come to feel a fool, thrashing around for wealth, trying to level people out, pushing people about. I felt tired and

81

resentful and angry. And now I see my political thinking was wrong, I took a wrong line, I had the wrong objectives, and far from feeling bitter or betrayed, I just feel . . . the knot is untied and I can look at the very same village, the very same people, I can look at the very same facts and I feel happy and hopeful.

(*A silence. Then noiselessly* HOU *returns with* CH'EN.)

CH'EN: You wanted to see me.

LITTLE LI: Yes. (*Pause.*) I felt . . . the policy had changed.

CH'EN: No.

LITTLE LI: You changed the policy.

CH'EN: No. (*Pause.*) The policy has always been the same. 'Depend on the poor peasants, unite with the middle peasants, destroy the feudal system.' That has always been the policy, is still the policy, and will be the policy in places where the feudal system has not been uprooted. Here it has been uprooted. That we got wrong.

LITTLE LI: We?

CH'EN: That we got wrong.

LITTLE LI: We? We didn't get it wrong. You got it wrong. (*Silence.*)
You got it wrong. I want to hear you say 'I take the blame.' (*Pause.*) Last time we were here you criticized us for arresting Yu-lai. But it was you who approved the arrest in the first place. (*Pause.*) Say the words 'I take the blame.'

CH'EN: Each level of leaders does its best to understand overall policy and apply it locally. If you are given a theory you must test it in practice. If it fails in practice it is up to you to send it back. Everyone must be active. Everyone must think all the time.

LITTLE LI: 'I take the blame.' Say it. (*Pause.*)

CH'EN: Primary responsibility for this last mistake rests with us at County headquarters. I take the blame. (*Silence.*)

LITTLE LI: You're just saying it. (CH'EN *raises his hands.*)

LITTLE LI: You're just saying it to get me back to work.

HOU: Li, you're behaving like a child.

CH'EN: It's not relevant.

LITTLE LI: I thought it was justice, I thought we were interested in justice.

CH'EN: Not as an abstract, as a practical thing. We've done what we can. From now on everyone's improvement must depend on production, on their new land, their new tools. If we'd gone on trying to equalize we'd have destroyed even that. Land reform can't be a final solution to men's problems. Land reform is just a step opening the way to socialism. And socialism itself is transitional. All we've done these past few years is give as many people as possible land to work. But our political choices have still to be made. Is each man now to work for himself? Is the pistol fired and the race underway, everyone climbing on each other's back? Or are we to build mutual aid, exchange labour, create property in common, hold the land collectively so we can all prosper together? You see the question has barely been asked. We haven't begun. (*Pause.*) You must go back.

HOU: Yes.

CH'EN: You must explain our mistakes, the people will be perfectly happy to listen. Tell the people the truth and they will trust you. One day, some time, this is the hardest thing, they will tell you the truth in return.
Tell them why China must be bold in concept but gentle in execution. Tell them . . . they are makers of the revolution every one.
They have lived already through many mistakes, but these are just ripples on the surface of the broad yellow river. Go back. Tell them.

SECTION TWELVE

I

A musical note, low, sustained.
   Village life. Dawn. The village at work. The work team return.

They look about the village. People hoeing.

    They begin to stop people one by one. Simultaneous dialogue based on the following in each different part of the stage.

You're going to have to give back . . .

Give back?

Yes, it's difficult to explain, let me explain, let me try to explain, there are good reasons.

(*and*)

I'm afraid there's been a change of policy. We've been to Lucheng.

I see.

It's best to tell you. I'd like to tell you . . .

(*and*)

We think it's best if you know exactly what's happening, there's been a change of policy.

Yes.

A good change, I think, but it sounds . . . hard on the surface anyway let me explain.

(*and*)

I'd like to explain to you what happened at Lucheng and then you tell me what you think. It'll need some thinking about.

(*As they talk the musical note turns into a superb massive groundswell of music that consumes the stage. Banners flood down so that the whole stage is surrounded in red. At the centre the cadres mutter on, gesturing, explaining, trying to hold the peasants' attention, getting a variety of first responses. Just before they are drowned out each cadre gets to the question*):

I'd like to know what you think.

What do you think?

Tell me.

Let me know what you think.

What do you think about this?

(*Then they drown in sound and light.*)

2

(*A single peasant. Hoeing in the field, as at the beginning.* HOU *boxes*

84

the compass from the tower: 'There will be a meeting.')

PEASANT:

    There is no Jade Emperor in heaven
    There is no Dragon King on earth
    I am the Jade Emperor
    I am the Dragon King
    Make way for me you hills and
       mountains
    I'm coming.

(*He goes to the meeting. The banner round the theatre unfurls the words of the poem.*)